Introduction

Part One of this book is dedicated to helping small business leaders understand their employees, because how any one individual learns is a large portion of what we all need to master in our roles as trainers. Having said that, anyone who teaches or trains others – no matter what the field – will find the book helpful because the concepts covered are both relevant and easily transferable. By the time you reach the end, you will know how to effectively communicate with your employees and help them through the entire learning process until they develop skill mastery.

How we train and develop our employees and the types of professional relationships we build with those who enter our sphere of influence are critical to our ability to impact and educate others. This has a direct effect on the operation and success of our businesses. Ultimately, knowing how to accurately assess our employees' skills and knowledge – without intimidation – while creating a safe and trusting learning environment will empower us to help them reach an elevated level of competence.

In Part Two of the book, we will look at the role of mentor and coach and how these roles are defined, as well as focus on the skills needed to be an engaging, effective coach and trainer. I have also laid out the actual On Task Skill Coaching™ process I recommend for conducting on-the-job training. This, supported by your new teaching knowledge, covered in Chapter Two, will ensure you will soon be well on your way to shaping and changing the lives of those you work with.

Before we start though, I would like to spend a few minutes with you so we are all on the same page in terms of what training, teaching and learning actually mean, as it is important for us to understand the differences between the three, as well as their most applicable uses.

Training What and When

Training is not an event, whereby an employee attends a training session one day and their boss expects the desired behavior (i.e. what has been trained and, hopefully, learned) the next. Training is actually a process. It begins before we even plan our first class or workshop and continues until the new knowledge, skills, and attitudes are applied regularly and competently in the workplace.

Many years ago, I was a corporate director of training for a large international company. I fulfilled this role across multiple units on three different continents. Part of my role was helping develop future company leaders and putting into place a corporate structure and a culture of ongoing learning and development. One of the first components of this was to analyze what training and development was already taking place, and what needed to change.

From my experience, I identified numerous reasons why management initiates employee training. The most common of these is poor work performance. In most cases, however, this is because a more structured and strategic approach to training is lacking. If your organization has a culture of employee development, service excellence and operational efficiency, then it probably has an ongoing approach to workplace training and advancement, and thus a more proactive approach to performance management.

Training is necessary in any of the scenarios detailed below but before you can plan any kind of program, you must first establish why the training is to take place.

Ask yourself:

1. Is there a skill gap between low- and high performing employees?
2. Are there opportunities for service improvements as identified through client satisfaction reports?
3. Are there new services or products being implemented that require supportive skill training or knowledge?
4. Are there new standard operating procedures that employees need to be aware of to ensure legal compliance?

TRAINING   small
BIG *for* BUSINESSES

Maximize your business performance by becoming your own training department. Effectively teach new skills, transfer knowledge and change problematic behaviors to create well-trained staff with a winning attitude

Niki Tudge

Table of Contents

5. Have individual employees been earmarked for career progression and, if so, are future development needs being addressed?

6. Do company downsizing initiatives require employees to be cross trained as part of a workplace flexibility or efficiency initiative?

Each of these reasons requires that employees learn new skills, acquire supplemental knowledge or make a shift in behavior, and thus necessitates workplace learning.

Learning Defined

All learning principles are predicated on a definition of learning, so let us do just that. Learning is a process, a journey that leads to change that occurs as a result of new experiences. Through these experiences comes an increased potential for improved performance and future learning.

Ambrose, Bridges, Lovett, DiPietro, & Norman (2010) present that there are three critical components here:

1. Learning is a process rather than a product.

2. Learning must involve a change in knowledge, beliefs, behaviors or attitudes.

3. Learning is not something to be pushed onto students, but is a direct result of how students interpret and respond to their experiences.

Learning has also been defined as the process of increasing one's capacity to take action and the process by which a person acquires new knowledge, skills and capabilities. Honey (1998), as quoted by Armstrong, declared learning as complex and various, covering a range of components, such as knowledge, skills, insights, beliefs, values, attitudes and habits (Armstrong, 2003, p. 538). In each of these definitions, keywords such as "process" and "acquires" are used. The definitions focus on the critical aspects of the learning process in terms of Experiential Learning Theory, making it more about adaptation than content. We will review *experiential learning* in more detail later on when we look at our training implementation system.

To Teach or To Train?

Whether we train, teach, or both, what are we ultimately impacting? Buckingham and Coffman (1999) differentiate between skills, knowledge and talent and propose that, together, they form the three elements of any one person's performance. The dissimilarity between the three is that, while skills can be trained and knowledge taught, talent can be neither. Skills are the "how-to" and knowledge is what one is aware of, cognitively speaking. Talent is a different phenomenon altogether, however, and cannot be taught. Rather, it is a repetitive behavior or action intrinsic to an individual's natural ability.

In contrast to Coffman and Buckingham, Ulrich and Smallwood (2012) assert that talent is not a singular phenomenon, but relies instead on a formula of competence × commitment × contribution. As trainers, we need to be sufficiently self-aware to be able to place an emphasis on the areas where we can have the most impact. Ideally, our work should single out the development of skills through effective training and the transfer of knowledge through teaching activities. The assumption is that if we are effective trainers and skilled teachers, then our students will, in turn, be able to enhance their knowledge and improve their skills. As a result, they will experience the learning process.

Let us now take a few minutes to look a little deeper at training versus teaching. Upon examination of the relevant literature, it becomes apparent that teaching is theoretically oriented, whereas training has more of a practical application. Teaching facilitates new knowledge, while training helps those who already have the knowledge to learn the tools and techniques required to apply it. Teaching penetrates minds, while training shapes habits and skills. Teachers provide information and knowledge, while trainers facilitate learning. Or, as Trumbull (1890) states: "It has been said that the essence of teaching is causing another to know." It may similarly be said that "the essence of training is causing another to do." (Rao, 2008).

Training is an interactive activity that helps us to perform skills. It requires learning by doing and experiencing practical activities (Pollice, 2003). In my opinion, and stated across relevant literature, training focuses on skills and narrows the focus, possibly over a shorter period of time. Typically, we also associate training with repetitive learning until we achieve competency and the skill becomes second nature. A select review of the literature discussing teaching suggests that, in contrast to training, the search of, or transfer of, knowledge is deeper and broader, and takes place over a longer period of time. We often say learning is a lifelong occupation.

Essentially, the goals associated with teaching and training are different, but I am not suggesting the two roles are mutually exclusive. On the contrary, it is important we balance our roles between teaching and transferring knowledge, and training and getting the job done.

I conclude here that training is a subset of teaching. The table on the following page highlights some of the topics that we, within our scope as trainers, will touch on when teaching employees. It differentiates between topics that require skill training or hands-on competency, and those that require teaching or the transfer of knowledge. I think it is fair to say most of these teaching activities would be best taught alongside compatible skill training exercises.

Examples of Skill Training

To train = to form by instruction, to make prepared for a skill.

- ✓ How to transfer a client call.
- ✓ How to invoice a client.
- ✓ How to use the company email.

Examples of Knowledge Teaching

To teach = to cause to know something, to guide the studies, impart the knowledge, to instruct

- ✓ Company orientation.
- ✓ Fire policy.
- ✓ Uniform standard.

Training versus Knowledge Teaching

The Model

A *learning theory* is a framework in which skills and knowledge are processed during the learning experience. To be effective as trainers we need to acquire the necessary people training and teaching skills. First, though, we must determine which learning theory model and process is most relevant to our application.

Since their inception, career and technical colleges have embraced experiential learning as the methodology of choice. Educational institutes such as these focus on preparing students with technical skills that will appeal to potential employers. Kolb (2015, p.1) states that: "judged by the standards of construct validity, Experiential Learning Theory has been widely accepted as a useful framework for…lifelong learning."

I believe the experiential learning model is most relevant to our learning theory application of teaching, and there are two contexts within the process that I believe apply and integrate perfectly into our roles as organizational trainers.

- The first is where students are given the opportunity to learn by applying knowledge and skills in a germane setting that is closely aligned to where the real application of learned knowledge and skills will take place. This direct encounter requires the student's active engagement to learn the skill.

- The second context involves applying the knowledge and improved skills acquired, based on the student's reflections from direct participation and direct encounters during everyday, real-life settings.

To explain more succinctly:

- Context one represents the formal training environment one provides through workplace training sessions.

- Context two represents the everyday management and coaching of employees in their workplace.

Much of my motivation for experiential learning stems from a negative opinion of training which is overly informative, trainer regulated, and involves a discipline-controlled delivery of new skills and knowledge.

Experiential learning is an adult-centric learning process where students develop skills and knowledge from direct experiences rather than in traditional classrooms or academic settings. In trainer speak, this means no more lectures or one-way training traffic.

As training professionals, we need to look at and be prepared to change how we deliver the necessary information to our employees, whether it is for the teaching of new skills or the active engagement of differing philosophies and methods. Experiencing something is an osmosis of action and thought, the bridge that connects an employee to the object they are interacting with. When we experience something, we do not separate the action from the end result. Each complements the other on a loop system.

Research proposes that anyone in a training or teaching role tends to implement whichever method they were taught. This means that, in the absence of a training certification program that focuses on teaching skills rather than just the transfer of knowledge, if most of an individual's learning experience was lecture-based, then that probably forms the foundation of how that individual now teaches their students (Wolvin, 1983).

Lecturing students is regarded as an easy and convenient method of teaching. It is a constructive model for communicating conceptual knowledge, particularly when there is a significant knowledge gap between the teacher and the students, and when there is a large audience. During lectures the teacher only has to focus on covering his or her program content and not on whether the student is actually learning anything or not. This type of teaching has been in play for over 800 years and remains a traditional method for many universities. Lecturing was, of course, the teaching method of choice and even necessity prior to the development of the first text books. As a convenient concept, lecturing is entrenched into our system of knowledge dissemination. As we already know though, convenient is not always the most effective option.

Studies discussed by Wolvin (1983) showed that a student's attention and focus wane after just 10 minutes during lectures and presentations. Thus, when a teacher exposes students to high-level lectures over sustained periods of time, it can undermine the student's ability to differentiate between what is truly salient versus what is not. This is similar to the so-called *redundancy effect* identified by cognitive overload researchers. One study showed that, when questioned halfway through a lecture, 55 percent of students said that their minds had wandered (Wolvin, 1983).

In many cases, experiential learning is self-explanatory. The student has to be directly involved in the learning experience and not just at the receiving end of a lecture or presentation. I cannot imagine how we could teach and train employees to do their jobs without them being extremely involved in the process. I am sure Founding Father Benjamin Franklin had experiential learning on his mind when he wrote: "Tell me and I forget, teach me and I remember, involve me and I will learn."

"I hear and I forget, I see and I remember, I do and I understand."

– Confucius

"Tell me and I forget, teach me and I remember, involve me and I will learn."

– Benjamin Franklin

"There is an intimate and necessary relation between the process of actual experience and education."

– John Dewey

PART ONE

Who Are Our Employees?

Understanding Our Employees

If we are committed to implementing a quality training process to transform our workplace into one of purpose and productivity, then it makes sense to educate ourselves on how to be effective trainers. Equally, if we are really dedicated to training and transforming our employees in ways that benefit them personally and professionally, it makes sense to know as much about them as possible.

Human beings have, in general, an intrinsic desire to understand other people, their emotions, their thought processes, and thus, their actions. We no longer need to worry about being chased and killed by saber-toothed tigers and our survival no longer depends on our abilities to run fast, climb a tree or throw a spear. Instead, we survive "based on our abilities to detect the needs and intentions of those around us. Our primary environment has become other people." (Cozolino, 2015, p. 13).

Because this is so important to us we tend to label people whenever we lack understanding. Understanding them, however, can help reduce the level of uncertainty we might feel about meeting and interacting with them. Our own uncertainties can cause us to make false assumptions about how our employees or trainees will react or behave towards us which, in turn, affects how we behave towards them. This is a damaging, dangerous and unnecessary cycle.

A key part of our effectiveness as trainers is being able to interact positively with our employees. This means we must present ourselves as accessible professionals and communicate appropriately with all team members.

When meeting new people, we perceive and interpret stimuli based on our sensory impressions. A cycle of perception and behavior follows and, if we get it wrong, can lead us to fundamentally misunderstand others' motives, goals and actions. As individuals, we tend to apply identification rules to the moods, attitudes and intentions of others from the stimuli we receive. In other words, we stereotype. All of us do it to some extent. Once we have created these inaccuracies and drawn our own conclusions, we then expect others to behave in certain ways. This not only affects how we treat them but also how we communicate with them. Instead, we should be treating everyone with respect, fairness, integrity and – yes – interest. If we are to coach others effectively, we need to be invested in them as individuals, not just their goals.

> *"I never teach my pupils; I only attempt to provide the conditions in which they can learn."*
> – Albert Einstein

Learning and Behavior - The Power of Reinforcement

As trainers and managers, we really should understand a little about the science of learning and behavior before we embark on the actual process. What is learning? What is behavior? How do either of these relate to our role as a coach and trainer?

Behavior can be overt or covert. Overt behavior is anything an individual does that can be observed and measured. In other words, any visible behavior you can see and can be directly impacted through training. Covert behaviors, on the other hand, are hidden and unobservable by anyone on the outside. They include actions like thinking and imagining.

Behaviors are also voluntary or involuntary. Voluntary behaviors are called *operants* and are strengthened or weakened by their consequences. This takes place through a process known as *operant conditioning*. In operant conditioning, both the type of reinforcement (i.e. the consequence or reward) and its delivery schedule are hugely important as these are the factors that impact the actual behavior.

Involuntary behaviors, also known as respondent behaviors, are elicited due to a person's emotional reaction to a situation. In a process known as *respondent conditioning* (or *classical conditioning*), the presence of one stimulus begins to reliably predict the presence of a second stimulus. As a result, the association, through conditioning, starts to affect how a person responds emotionally to the first, eliciting stimulus. If the conditioning process is aversive, an initial pleasant or happy emotional response can change into a *negative conditioned emotional response*, such as fear or anxiety. It can work the other way around too, in that a negative emotional response can be changed to one of happiness and joy, i.e. a *positive conditioned emotional response*.

What is Conditioning?

Conditioning is a process of changing behavior.

This graphic shows how a *neutral stimulus*, through conditioning, becomes a *conditioned stimulus* that elicits a *conditioned response*.

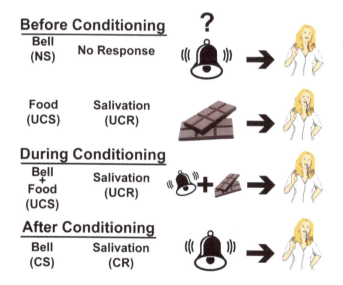

Key:

NS = Neutral Stimulus

UCS = Unconditioned Stimulus

UCR = Unconditioned Response

CS = Conditioned Stimulus

CR = Conditioned Response

Now that you have looked at the graphic, the following text may help you understand this concept.

Within an organism there are two types of reflexes (or responses): *unconditioned* and *conditioned*.

1. An *unconditioned reflex* (UR) is unlearned and occurs unconditionally

2. A *conditioned reflex* (CR) is acquired and considered impermanent.

An unconditioned reflex consists of an *unconditioned stimulus* (US) and an *unconditioned response* (UR).

- An unconditioned stimulus is something that, when presented, evokes a natural, unconditioned, response, such as blinking when air is blown towards the eyelid, or sweating when stressed or scared.

- Unconditioned reflexes are important for an animal's survival.

- Food is an example of a US and a person's drooling is an example of the resulting UR.

A conditioned reflex occurs when a conditioned stimulus (CS) creates a conditioned response (CR).

- This is a learned response to a given set of conditions occurring in the environment.

- Pioneering Russian psychologist Ivan Pavlov recognized that any stimulus could become a conditioned stimulus when paired repeatedly with an unconditioned stimulus.

Now here is the important part. Respondent conditioning takes place when an unconditioned stimulus that elicits an unconditioned response is repeatedly paired with a neutral stimulus. As a result of conditioning, the neutral stimulus becomes a conditioned stimulus that reliably elicits a conditioned response. Each single pairing is considered a trial. In respondent conditioning, the presentation of the two stimuli (neutral and unconditioned) occurs regardless of the behavior the individual is exhibiting. The behavior elicited is a reflex response (Chance, 2008, p.64).

Another aspect of respondent conditioning is called *higher order conditioning*. Higher order conditioning takes place when a well-established condi-tioned stimulus is paired with a neutral stimulus to elicit a conditioned response. It takes place in the absence of an unconditioned stimulus, and many more stimuli can come to elicit conditional responses, not just those paired with an unconditioned stimulus. This enhances our adaptation and survival ability. But higher order conditioning also affects and influences many emotional reactions, such as fear. We should thus be aware of it in the workplace. (Chance, 2008).

This graphic below shows how a neutral stimulus, through high order conditioning (also called second order conditioning), becomes a condi-tioned stimulus that elicits a conditioned response. For those of us who have pets, we see this every day at meal times when we go into the kitchen and open a cabinet or reach for a pet bowl.

Higher Order/Second Order Conditioning

The wonderful thing about *respondent conditioning* is that when we grasp the scientific principles behind it, we can then use it in the workplace and our training lessons to modify a trainee's behavior. The graphic below shows how conditioning can be used to create a pleasant or enjoyable response to a stimulus. This conditioning process is called *counterconditioning*.

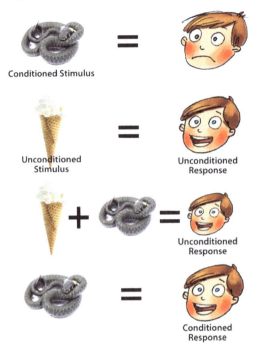

An Example of Operant Conditioning

Let's say a competent and highly-trained employee performs to an excellent standard and clients provide gratuities accordingly. Each time a specific client service is reinforced with a gratuity, the employee's likelihood of repeating that same standard of client service will be strengthened. In other words, the behavior has been strengthened by its consequences. The behavior has been positively reinforced.

An Example of Respondent Conditioning

Say a manager's appearance in a certain office or department has been paired continually with overly critical feedback to the employees. This will more than likely condition a problematic emotional response be-cause, whenever the manager appears, it elicits a feeling of anxiety – or similar – in the staff.

An Example of How Respondent and Operant Conditioning Work Together – The Gordian Knot

To continue with the above example, when the manager appears and staff experience anxiety due to what has become a conditioned emotional response (i.e. respondent conditioning), the manager may well start to feel unwelcome as staff busy themselves or find other ways to avoid talking to him. As a consequence of their behavior, the manager may quickly leave the area. The employees' overt avoidance behavior (i.e. operant conditioning) has been successful in relieving their source of anxiety. As a result, the behavior has been reinforced, which strengthens the likelihood of the manager being slighted in future visits.

What is a Gordian Knot?

A Gordian Knot is something that is very difficult to separate

It is important to be aware that all behavior is a product of its environment and can be modified either through operant or respondent conditioning protocols. If you specifically wish to build or strengthen new skills with your employees, you will need to use operant conditioning protocols to help them acquire and strengthen the behaviors related to building those new skills.

For example, if you have an employee that needs some attitude adjustment or has problematic emotional responses to certain tasks, situations or people, then you can leverage your new-found knowledge of respondent conditioning protocols to support behavior change. Your challenge here will be to help the person reframe the emotions triggered by a certain task, situation or individual. Just recognize that you are not a behavior counselor and make sure you only work within the parameters of your expertise and the requirements of your training role.

Most of what we will focus on modifying and changing will be unconstructive, overt, operant behaviors that do not promote a safe, productive and positive work environment. We will also use motivation and *positive reinforcement to* build new skills and behaviors. (*Note: We will cover the concept of positive reinforcement in more detail later on.*)

Through the actions and words we use to motivate and manage, we can influence what our employees think and how they feel about their jobs and their workplace, and we must remain aware of this. We do not want to become a stimulus that reliably predicts an unpleasant experience or training session. Rather, we want to be a stimulus that predicts fun, enjoyment, workplace development and a feeling of confidence and well-being. This is respondent conditioning at its best – one stimulus reliably predicts another and then conditioning takes place.

When we train our employees, we expect them to learn. To be sure though, we need to see that learning has taken place. Learning is a measurable change in behavior due to experience. If our interpretation of learning is defined by a change in cognitive structure or a change in the nervous system, we must infer that learning has taken place, although we would not be able to define or measure it. Learning does not impact how our employees behave; it impacts their ability to modify their behavior given a different set of events (Chance, 2008).

There are two main **functions** *to behavior:*

1) To gain access to a reinforcer.

2) **To** *escape or avoid a punisher.*

Functional *means that the behavior is purposeful or useful for the student.*

As trainers, we want to create change and improve existing skills, and diminish inappropriate behavior or behavior sets (i.e. groups of similar behaviors) so we can help employees improve their own performance and thus that of the business.

Evolution has an important place in learning. Influenced by natural selection and adaptive behaviors, it references the change in traits of a population over a period of time. By the same token, if employees cannot learn and adapt within their work environment, there is a good chance they may miss out on workplace advancement opportunities, promotions or performance-related pay increases. Conversely, ongoing inadequate work performance or a poor work attitude can result in a demotion or even termination.

There is an interaction between genetics and the environment that molds behavior and ensures survival and reproduction of the species. Genes and learning form equal parts of the same continuum. Therefore, in our small businesses, we need to ensure our recruitment policies attract and secure the right individuals with the right traits and personality. We need employees who instinctively like to work in teams, like to succeed, want to help others, and are reliable and trustworthy. If these qualities are already in place, all we have to do is teach and train any other necessary skills through effective on-the-job programs such as On Task Skill Coaching™.

In my opinion, learning takes place in two different contexts. The first of these is *task-conscious* or *acquisition learning*, first documented by Rogers (2003). Acquisition learning is considered an ongoing process. It is concrete, immediate and confined to a specific activity, and is not concerned with general principles. Much of the learning involved in and around the workplace or the home environment is task-conscious, sometimes referred to as unconscious or implicit learning. In other words, the learner may not even be conscious of the fact that they are learning.

The second context references learning-conscious, or formalized, learning. This refers to learning that takes place in a formal training environment and arises from the process of facilitated learning. It is "educative learning" rather than the accumulation of experience. To this extent, there is a consciousness during training whereby employees are aware that the task they are engaged in entails attaining knowledge or new skills. Formalized training sessions make learning more of a conscious task (Rogers, 2003). Therefore, learning-conscious learning involves guided episodes.

When approached in this way it becomes clear that these contrasting ways of learning can occur simultaneously. Both are usually present in an employee's living and working environment, and because of this it is important to manage and shape behaviors both inside the formal training session and throughout the workday. Effective training programs and an understanding of learning theory can help small business owners achieve this.

Several years ago, I developed a system of training for my national licensing company. The system, which I called ARRF©, is based on learning theory and provides an approach to management and relationship building that helps with employee development.

ARRF© stands for:

A = Active Involvement

Active involvement in the learning process is critical. When a trainee is actively participating rather than passively observing, greater learning takes place.

R = Repetition

Newly acquired skills need to be repeated frequently in a variety of contexts to ensure they are robust. This means the skills learned will be effective in all aspects of the work environment. Frequent repetition in various scenarios ensures the skill is truly owned: the employee cannot only generalize the behavior in new situations, but can also discriminate when it is appropriate to use the behavior.

R = Reward

Positive reinforcement in the form of rewards for accomplishing skills successfully is effective to ensure learning takes place. On-the-spot rewards can shape and direct employee behavior during training sessions, whereas promotions, incentives, workplace recognition and bonuses can be used as positive reinforcement for long-term behavior retention. As previously explained, positive reinforcement is the practice of rewarding desirable employee behavior in order to strengthen that behavior. For example, when you praise an employee for doing a good job, you increase the likelihood of him/her doing that job very well again. Positive reinforcement both shapes behavior and enhances your employee's self-image. Recognizing and rewarding desirable behavior is the key to motivating employees to work more productively and using this method will reap many benefits:

1. When used together with a training plan it helps clearly define and communicate expected behaviors and strengthens the connection between high performance and rewards.

2. With correct use and timing it reinforces an employee's behavior immediately. This helps when learning a new technique or behavior and promotes quick, thorough learning.

3. Not only does it reinforce behavior but it also motivates students to continue doing good work. A lack of positive feedback or positive reinforcement can lead to student dissatisfaction.

4. It increases workplace productivity by rewarding workers who help company leadership with supply and time management control.

5. Reinforced employees feel more confident and become eager to learn new techniques, take advanced training, and accept more responsibility in the workplace.

6. When used to reward employees who suggest improved work procedures it helps create a more innovative business environment.

7. Employees who receive recognition for their achievements are more enthusiastic about their work, more cooperative, and more open to change.

8. When you show appreciation and reward employees for good work, you increase their job commitment and workplace loyalty.

F = Finite Objectives

Clearly defined and attainable objectives make it clear to both trainer and employee what is to be taught and learned. With clear objectives, the student and instructor can easily recognize when a skill has been mastered. During the process, we train – test – train to ensure our objectives are met.

ARRF© evolved from an understanding of respondent and operant conditioning, and how we can utilize this scientific approach to train and manage employees in the workplace. Once in place, the components of management, training and relationship are then used to build solid employer-employee relationships and make sure the latter are consistently performing at a higher level.

The process entails managing the employees' environment to ensure it is conducive to empowering a high standard of performance. Strategic training programs and an educational approach to management mean employees are receptive and able to learn, and are supported throughout the learning process. If they are managed productively, trained at each job skill, and have a trusting and productive relationship with their peers and superiors, they will show huge potential and talent during their tenure.

A very important component of ARRF© is rewarding the behaviors we want to encourage. In scientific terms, this is known as *positive reinforcement*, a topic I have touched on before but is important enough to warrant further explanation.

> *"The consequences of an act affect the probability of its occurring again." – B. F. Skinner*

The Operant Conditioning Quadrants

Positive reinforcement is one of the *four quadrants* of operant conditioning. As previously explained, operant conditioning is so called because the behavior operates on the environment.

The four quadrants of operant conditioning are:

- *Negative reinforcement.*
- *Positive reinforcement.*
- *Negative punishment.*
- *Positive punishment.*

The Four Quadrants of Operant Conditioning

The terms positive and negative do not describe the consequence of the behavior, but indicate whether a stimulus has been added (positive) or subtracted (negative) to increase or weaken the preceding behavior.

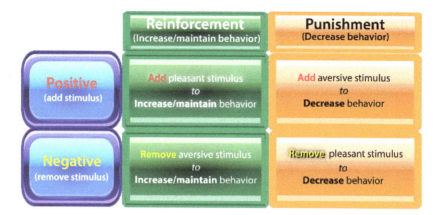

	Reinforcement (Increase/maintain behavior)	Punishment (Decrease behavior)
Positive (add stimulus)	**Add** pleasant stimulus *to* **Increase/maintain** behavior	**Add** aversive stimulus *to* **Decrease** behavior
Negative (remove stimulus)	**Remove** aversive stimulus *to* **Increase/maintain** behavior	**Remove** pleasant stimulus *to* **Decrease** behavior

- Two of the quadrants of operant conditioning strengthen behaviors and are referred to as *reinforcements*.

- The other two quadrants weaken behavior and are referred to as *punishments*.

Both positive and negative reinforcement increase the strength of a behavior due to the consequences.

- With positive reinforcement, a behavior is followed by the appearance, or an increase in the intensity, of a desirable stimulus. The reason this stimulus is referred to as positive reinforcement is because it is something the subject seeks out, or will work to get (e.g. public recognition, a pay rise, verbal praise). As a result, it reinforces the behavior that precedes it.

- With negative reinforcement, a behavior is strengthened by the ability to avoid or escape an aversive stimulus (e.g. being publicly reprimanded, loss of overtime). As such, negative reinforcement is sometimes referred to as *escape-avoidance learning*.

A reinforcing experience must have three characteristics to qualify as reinforcement:

1. The behavior must have a consequence.
2. The behavior must increase in strength.
3. The increase in strength must be a result of the consequence (Chance, 2008).

As behavior is the function of its consequences, and whereas reinforcement strengthens the likelihood of a behavior, then punishment reduces the strength of a behavior. Punishers are aversive and something an employee will seek to avoid or escape.

- When an aversive event is added to a situation, then positive punishment has taken place.
- Negative punishment subtracts something from the situation, like privileges, and is sometimes called *penalty training.*

Again, as with reinforcers, a punishment experience must have three characteristics to qualify as punishment:

1. The behavior must have a consequence.
2. The behavior must decrease in strength.
3. The reduction in strength must be a result of the consequence (Chance, 2008).

All this information begs the question: How does a basic knowledge of operant conditioning strengthen your skills as a trainer?

Analysis of Behavior Change Based on Postcedent Environment

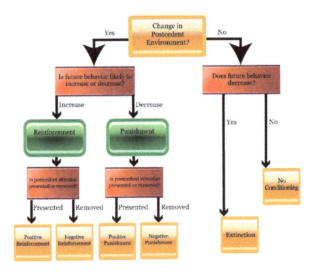

As trainers, we need to understand the science and theory of learning and behavior so we can correctly use the principles to motivate, teach and reinforce new skills. If we understand this science, and how to carefully select and use reinforcement, we can build a non-punitive work environment that supports employee growth and performance. We cannot just assume it is reinforcing for employees if we do something we think is nice. We must ask ourselves, has the behavior we targeted for reinforcement increased and was the behavior increase a result of the consequence? If so, then positive reinforcement has taken place.

The chart above shows how we can functionally analyze what has happened based on a change in the *postcedent environment*. In other words, after a training or behavior intervention, we can ask ourselves whether the students' behavior increased or decreased as a result of our influence and whether a stimulus was removed or presented. The answers will help us confirm whether our intervention was positive reinforcement or negative punishment. We should work to avoid using negative reinforcement or positive punishment as this would indicate that we are applying or manipulating aversive stimuli. This is not an ethical approach to our training sessions and certainly not conducive to stress-free, enjoyable learning.

The Two- and Three-Term Contingencies

There is much more to the theory of operant and respondent conditioning that will help us understand our role as a trainer, an employee's role as a trainee, and the learning process itself. Throughout the book, wherever it is relevant, I will include these concepts and outline them so they are easily understood.

In operant conditioning, the *three-term contingency* refers to the relationship between the *antecedent stimulus*, the *behavior* and the *consequence*. In respondent conditioning, the *two-term contingency* refers to the relationship between the two *antecedent stimuli*. The graphic below shows how these contingencies work and the difference between the two.

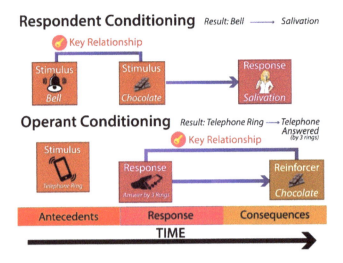

What is Reinforcement?

As previously discussed, reinforcement is something a person seeks to obtain, and it something they will work for. This could be verbal praise, personal recognition, a bonus or one of many other options. The value of the reinforcer depends on the employee. Some employees enjoy being publicly recognized, while others would find this very punishing or unpleasant. Primary reinforcers, or unconditioned reinforcers, are in-trinsically rewarding in that we do not have to learn to like them. They are biologically important and intrinsic to our survival, such as food, air, safety, and security.

Reinforcers that we come to learn as being of value due to their having been paired with a primary reinforcer are known as *secondary reinforcers*. It is purely through conditioning that we learn to value them. Take a dollar bill for example. We learn very quickly, as children, that money gives us access to lots of things we really want. Conditioned reinforcers, such as cash, can be used in many situations and have been paired with many different kinds of reinforcement. These are referred to as *generalized reinforcers* (Chance, 2008, p. 136). All secondary reinforcers, or conditioned reinforcers, owe their effectiveness directly or indirectly to primary reinforcers (Chance, 2008, p.135).

Schedules of Reinforcement

When using positive reinforcement, it is not only important to find the correct reinforcement, i.e. one that is of high value to the employee, but to understand how and when to use it. There are many different possi-ble schedules of reinforcement and I have highlighted below the ones I think are most commonly used in the workplace.

Continuous reinforcement means a behavior is reinforced each time it oc-curs, i.e. a schedule of one reinforcer for one response. Because each behavior is reinforced the increase in the rate of behavior is rapid. Con-tinuous reinforcement is rare in a natural environment where most behavior is reinforced on an *intermittent schedule* (Pierce & Cheney, 2004, p.124).

With intermittent schedules of reinforcement only some, not all, behav-ioral responses are reinforced. *Intermittent schedules include ratio schedules of reinforcement and interval schedules of reinforcement.*

Ratio schedules of reinforcement are based on a set number of responses given prior to reinforcement whereas *interval schedules* operate on a set amount of time having passed prior to reinforcement being delivered. Both ratio and interval schedules can be on a fixed or a variable, random schedule of reinforcement (Pierce & Cheney, 2004).

Other schedules of reinforcement include duration schedules and *time schedules*. Duration schedules of reinforcement are contingent on a be-havior being performed for a period of time. A *fixed duration schedule* requires the behavior be performed for a set period of time whereas a *variable duration schedule* works around some average. Each performance of behavior is reinforced after a different du-ration. The graph below shows the schedules of *fixed ratio*, *variable ratio*, *fixed interval* and *variable interval* schedules.

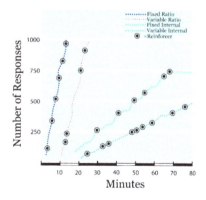

Possible Reinforcement Schedules

If we are to train and influence the behavior of others, then we need to understand what motivates and drives them. The secret to understanding people depends on our ability to communicate effectively. Words are very powerful tools and the choices we make can influence their thoughts, attitudes and behaviors.

By paying close attention to the language our employees use we can get a greater insight into what they are really trying to say. We may have to query them and dig deeper to truly understand their challenges and goals, but if we understand their language we can respond more appropriately and effectively to them as individuals. This will certainly enhance our role as coach and cheerleader.

In real time, how many of us actually listen and pay attention to an employee's every word without the distraction of other things in our environment or our own thoughts? In this stimulus-driven world where we have data flying at us from all directions, many of us have developed poor habits when it comes to communicating with those we spend a lot of time with, such as our families and work colleagues. In many cases, important communication often gets thrown about at inappropriate times while we partake in other activities or are multitasking.

The saying "two ears and one mouth" sums up part of our role as communicators: ask questions and then listen carefully to understand more. If we recognize that listening carefully is crucial to effective communication, we must accept that important communication needs to take place in an

What is Hearing vs. Listening?

Hearing is a passive activity. To really understand what is being said, one must actually try. Be present in the conversation and really listen to each of the words and the entire message.

What is Appreciative Inquiry?

Appreciative inquiry is the art of seeking information about the things that we value.

Appreciative inquiry focuses on what is right and how we can make it better. It is an enlightened way to approach employee communication and fact finding.

environment where this is possible, not on a shop floor or in the middle of production or customer service areas.

When we hear, we perceive sounds from our environment. When we listen, however, we actually identify those stimuli. Of course, listening involves extra effort on our part. To really understand what we have heard we must take extra steps, such as giving employees our undivided attention and being present in the moment with them. If we take the time to do this, the impact it can have on developing a clearer and more effective relationship with them will be enormous.

Ultimately, the process of communicating is about exchanging information. As trainers, we must ensure we gain access to every detail we can, whether as part of our initial employee assessment or during the training process. We will come back to this later when we look at experiential learning and how we can optimize our training using this scientific theory, coupled with a strategic training process using positive reinforcement.

Asking questions and using appreciative inquiry to gain insight into knowledge of value is extremely important. Well-crafted questions will help us create more engaging conversations that reveal important and insightful information. When we communicate positively, it also lets our employees know we are truly interested in them. Asking questions of people who are shy or concerned about making a mistake will help empower them and bring them into the learning process.

There are many different reasons to ask questions. Maybe we want to help employees feel at ease or motivate them to engage in a discussion. We may want to encourage them to actively partcipate or move the focus elsewhere. In other instances our questions may aim to inspire a

> *"Words are singularly the most powerful force available to humanity. We can choose to use this force constructively with words of encouragement, or destructively using words of despair. Words have energy and power with the ability to help, to heal, to hinder, to hurt, to harm, to humiliate and to humble."*
>
> *– Yehuda Berg*

connection or establish how much they know and understand from a prior training session.

Questions also help employees reflect on training sessions or learning experiences, which helps them conceptualize what they are learning and how best they can apply it. We must therefore engage with them so we can understand their experiences and needs. By taking the opportunity to communicate with confidence, we have the ability to influence, persuade and make an impact regarding their knowledge, skills and attitude. Positive communication breeds self-confidence, credibility and productiveness. It explains the relevant points and filters out the polite but unnecessary fillers. Our aim should be to provide employees with the salient points only, the bare bones, the ideas, thoughts and opinions that make sense to them while promoting the best of intentions. How we say things can be just as important as what we say. By changing the intonation of our voice we can inject emotions into our messages and make them sound either up- or downbeat. We can also modify our tone to help identify the purpose of a sentence. If we are asking a question, for example, the intonations are obviously different from when we are making a statement.

Why Should Verbal and Nonverbal Messages Always Be in Sync?

If we are not in control of our nonverbal skills, or if they are in direct conflict with our verbal message, then we cannot be sure exactly what we are communicating to our employees.

By changing which words or syllables we emphasize we can change the entire meaning of our message. We can also affect the clarity and effectiveness of our communication by altering the tempo of our speech. Speed and the use of appropriate pauses can actually change the meaning of the words spoken. If we talk too quickly it can be difficult for people to engage in a conversation with us and they may have problems deciphering what we say. If we speak too slowly we risk boring our audience. Our goal should be to set the pace at a tempo that is appropriate for the listener.

Volume should be kept at a moderate level. If we speak too softly it can indicate a lack of confidence and conviction in what we are trying to communicate. If we speak too loudly it may indicate anger or impatience. We do not have to have taken formal elocution lessons to articulate and enunciate words correctly. We can, however, make sure we pronounce words in a way that is generally accepted or understood. It is worth taking the time to develop one's pronunciation and enunciation skills. This will ensure we are accurately understood, particularly for those of us who like to cite industry nomenclature or scientific research.

Effective communication also includes body language that can support or refute what we are saying verbally. In many cases our body language communicates our mood before a single word is spoken. If we are upset or angry, aggravated or irritated, it does not matter how sweet our words sound. An employee will pick up on our physical gestures and this will negatively impact the message.

What Is Effective Communication?

Effective communication is our trump card and a tool in our kit that needs to be on permanent standby, fully flexed and ready to go

If we are not in control of our nonverbal skills or if they are in direct conflict with our verbal message, then we cannot be sure exactly what we are communicating to our employees and our intended message risks being lost.

Remember, body language refers to posture, facial expressions, gestures and movements, all of which convey their own messages. Research on the human brain shows that emotions manifest first in our body language before the rational brain catches up. Thus, if we are impatient or angry, our body language will reflect this before we have the chance to put words into action. By the same token, learning to read employees' body language is a useful skill which will help us understand their intents, if not their specific thoughts. Inconsistencies between verbal and nonverbal communication can result in much confusion and the delivery of an inaccurate message. As one who continuously asks herself, "What could I have done better?" I must believe that if I avail myself of these important communication tools, I can make great strides in my ability to communicate and educate others.

In our training environments, after we have an effective system in place, communication is our most powerful ally. It is our trump card and a tool in our kit that needs to be on permanent standby, fully flexed and ready to go. If we arc not prepared and do not have this ally alongside us, we will not have meaningful, engaging and impactful communication with our employees. As a result, we will never be able to effectively share our philosophy, goals, knowledge, skills and ideas.

Lacking shared meaning because of poor communication often forms the crux of many problems that occur between mentors and employees. This means the main avenue to success in any given training program is first improving and then strategically using our communication skills. I believe this directly impacts an employee's levels of commitment and compliance to the training process, both of which are much-needed attributes.

Building Productive Relationships

Perception describes the process by which we become aware of the outside world and ourselves. How we perceive others is very important and impacts how we communicate. We tend to distort our perceptions to fit our beliefs using our unique and individual stimulus-filtering system, consciously and subconsciously controlling it by only allowing certain stimuli through while other unimportant stimuli are filtered out.

The filtering process looks and works like this:

- Stimuli approach.
- Stimuli enter the filtering system and are selected as important or thrown out as useless.
- Stimuli are integrated and organized.
- Stimuli are translated into logic and meaning based on the individual's own biases.
- Based on this translation, the person thinks and takes action.

How we filter individual stimuli and how we think and act are products of our own individual experiences, assumptions and perceptions, which are affected and distorted by the following characteristics:

- **The Personal:** Values, beliefs, attitudes and expectations.
- **The Perceived:** Physical attributes, age, gender and nomenclature of the other person.
- **The Situation:** Location, setting, climate, etc.

By examining the ways in which we distort our perceptions we can work to avoid them. For example, when we put people into groups or categories such as gender, age or race, and then judge them accordingly, it is called *stereotyping*. There is also a phenomenon known as the *halo effect*, whereby we group people based on their interpersonal skills, smiles or other easily measured factors that we like. When we distort our opinions by using selective perception we tend to just focus on one aspect and ignore others that may be important.

We may also project our own needs and attributes onto people in situations where, if we perform poorly, we blame external events, but if others perform poorly, we blame them directly. Recognizing the ways in which our perceptions can be distorted is central to communicating effectively. To be an engaging, motivating and collaborative communicator we need to be aware of how we see others. When we are aware of this we can consciously work to change the distortions we create.

Once we understand our own perceptions and those of our employees we can begin to build productive relationships. In the process we are likely to find that employees are more committed and compliant with our coaching recommendations.

How does this all happen? How do we become so unique in our approach and behavior? First, we are all individuals, a combination of genetics and environment. Our genes define the sort of person we are in terms of body, mind and emotions, while our environment impacts our characteristics and behavior. Therefore, we are all unique. This takes us back to the science of learning, the difference between genes and natural selection, and our ability to learn from our environment. *Natural selection* helps humans adapt to change across generations but does not help us cope with fast environmental change. When we need to modify our behavior to adapt to new and changing environments, we must first learn how to do this.

Learning indicates a change in behavior and takes place through experience of events. i.e. stimuli. Learning is essential to our survival and comes into play after reflexes and modal action patterns have done their job (Chance, 2008).

What is Natural Selection, Modal Action Patterns and Reflexes?

Natural selection affects innate behaviors such as reflexes, modal action patterns and general behavior traits. The difference between reflexes and modal action patterns is that a reflex, the relationship between a specific event and specific response, only affects individual muscles and glands. Modal action patterns are an orderly sequence of reflex behaviors and affect the entire being. The role of genes in human behavior is defined as behavior traits. (Chance, 2008).

When communicating with our employees we need to treat them as individuals and recognize that they all have different needs, expectations and motivations. There is no one-size-fits-all communication style, no one tone of voice or canned message. How we communicate is key to creating a productive ambience in the workplace. We need to think about the climate we want and need to create. There is a formula for building open and honest communication that results in an environment of trust and collaboration. Honest communication creates not only an understanding about what is being said, but also the intention or emotion behind it. Hidden feelings, biases and assumptions cloud communication and prevent honesty and forthrightness.

The ideal work situation is one where everyone trusts each other, as well as the intentions, motivations and actions of all parties. If we can trust our employees, they will trust us in return. This allows us to build a climate of mutual trust and ensure excellent professional relationships. A productive team that can work together will thus emerge, creating a positive working environment for everyone concerned.

Appreciative Inquiry

One of the best ways to develop trust in the workplace is to use a system called Appreciative Inquiry (AI), which is detailed in the graphic below.

Appreciative Inquiry

Cooperrider et al. (2001, p.12) state that: "Appreciative Inquiry deliberately seeks to discover people's exceptionality – their unique gifts, strengths, and qualities. It actively searches and recognizes people for their specialties – their essential contributions and achievements. AI builds momentum and success because it believes in people." I interpret this to mean that, rather than focusing on how employees or peers may be negatively impacting your goals or action plans, think about how you can help them utilize their individual talents.

By implementing the AI Model to encourage self-reflection, self-worth and positive thought we should be able set a course of action that will leverage our employees' unique abilities and qualities to create a collaborative change for the better. This can only have a positive impact on our training goals, and can all be achieved through the art and application of asking positive and pertinent questions that focus on the possibilities and the shared vision.

How can we use AI in our businesses?

1. AI helps us focus on finding the best in people. For example, rather than zeroing in on the fact that an individual has a tendency to overthink and overanalyze we would focus on their creativity and how their contribution can positively impact the team and its goals. By concentrating on how and where they are successful, we can create greater possibilities for our overall success. This is the *what is*.

2. By using AI, we can create a more positive work environment that draws on individual potential and use it as another component of our success. If we are having challenges with an employee who is missing assignment deadlines or not being cooperative, then we can implement AI to help us appreciate their motivations and vision. With this newfound understanding we can further engage our employees, who will, in turn, be more committed and passionate because they will choose to participate in our training goals rather than feel they are being forced into them. This is the *what should be*.

3. When we remove the focus on negativity and criticism and instead work with our employees or peers to discover solutions that work for everyone, it creates a more engaging and empowering work environment. This change in culture from negative focus to possibilities and support will create diversity and action-centered team goals. This is the *what can be*.

The Appreciative Inquiry Model encompasses *positivity*, *inquiry* and *influence*, which is depicted in full in the graphic on the next page, but first I will explain.

Positivity

To start with, we must change the way we think. The application of positive thought to each and every situation is imperative to create an environment that harnesses change in people's behavior and attitudes. Positive attitudes create confidence and this will support future success.

When we feel positive we are better equipped to make changes in our own lives, and this removes us further from negative thoughts and situations that manifest as low motivation and a feeling of failure and despair. Thinking positively is also one of the easiest ways to help ourselves and others reduce personal stress.

The fastest way to destroy a positive attitude is to zero in on what can go wrong and what will happen if it does. Establishing positive goals and focusing on them is a principal component of AI. I am not suggesting that ignorance is bliss and we always need to be mindful of the other side of the equation, but we must acknowledge that we have as much, if not more, control when we are working towards the upside than if we are spiraling down into negativity. Even the trickiest problems are not all-or-nothing situations and this line of thinking needs to be avoided at all costs.

Get into the habit of using positive language with yourself and others. Avoid, "I cannot do that" or, "I will never finish this," and instead use language such as, "I can," "I will" and, "It is my intention to." This type of upbeat action language is contagious and needs to be shared alongside compliments and positive reinforcement for a job well done. Let others know they have succeeded at something or simply have a great attitude. Make it a habit to always reassure yourself and others of the value you have and the skills and abilities you can contribute to a team.

Using Appreciative Inquiry in Your Business

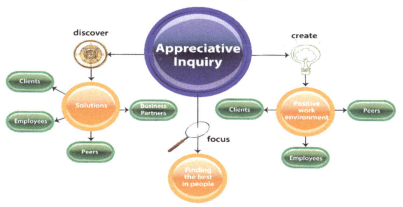

Inquiry

When it comes to conducting interviews for new staff, promotions or workplace problem-solving activities, the techniques used in AI are a far distance from traditional styles. Removing all the usual stereotypes, AI focuses instead on a 4-D approach, encompassing:

- **Discovery:** Identification and appreciation of what works.
- **Dream:** The process of what can be or what can be imagined to be.
- **Design:** The leveraging of what is best.
- **Destiny:** The delivery of new results.

Against this backdrop, an interviewee will be asked positive questions, encouraged to share pertinent stories and helped through a journey of discovery. They will be encouraged to think and envisage how they can contribute to the success of the situation. Scare tactics, fear, threats and intimidation are a thing of the distant past. How we approach the interview and the type of questions we ask will set the tone. Positive questions prompt positive answers. Sharing of experiences and opinions encourages empowerment and confidence, while genuine questions to seek mutual solutions develop trust and a feeling of safety and security.

During interviews, look for recurring themes. Patterns will emerge in an employee's experiences and how they narrate them. Themes such as expertise, trust, and commitment will become evident and this will help you build a sense and understanding of what is important to each individual. In turn, this will help you build a plan that encompasses shared values. For example, you can deduce that a person is loyal if they share how they saw a project through to the end, or stayed with a company even when times were tough. If they express how important it is for them to see ventures or goals through to completion, this may indicate that they have a high level of commitment. Using this 4-D cycle for one-on-one conversations can leverage knowledge, which stimulates creativity and builds a momentum toward change and a commitment to the process (Martinetz, 2002).

Influence

One of the key goals of using AI is to positively influence other people and create an impetus of change. This can have a ripple effect that starts off in small ways and gradually extends to more people and wider-ranging audiences. We can impact others through a change in our own behavior, as well as guide people toward changing their behavior by helping them see how competent and valued they are. By using AI, we make it possible for people to ask questions that seek to find alternative solutions and create possibilities. When this happens, there is no limit to the types of creativity and genius we can unleash in our work environment.

Our goal should always be to be more positive and upbeat, and to support others in their differences and celebrate these quirks. Use inquiry to generate visions, possibilities and expectations around shared goals. When people understand this, they are drawn to new and different ways of doing things, free from negativity and individual restrictions. When they have an idea of what is expected of them they will live up to these new and positive expectations. Create, then, an environment where you recognize and applaud the best in people. Not only will your employees benefit from knowing the individual qualities they contribute will be appreciated, but I can guarantee it will make you feel much better to surround yourself and interact with positive, supportive personalities.

To Influence We Must First Understand

While we do not have the power to control other people, we can always do our best to persuade them. If we wish to influence our employees, we must first set aside our personal point of view and look at the situation from their perspective. We cannot assume that because a philosophy or principle is clear to us that it is clear to them. If we can answer, "What is in it for me?" on the employee's behalf, then we are halfway there. Being able to answer this question will help us understand what is important to employees in terms of their values, interests and preferences. If we build bridges with them, we will be able to better understand them and make greater headway on building our credibility and trust as a coach and mentor. This translates to finding common ground and getting to "yes." This is the win-win formula.

Very few issues are black and white. In most professions we live and operate in a vast gray area. There are, of course, exceptions to this. In many companies, health and safety policies, financial controls and government mandates are black and white and non-negotiable. Most other areas, such as customer service and workplace practices, may only need to have mandated outputs but enable and empower the employees to work the process the way they deem most appropriate, based on the individual situation.

We cannot risk losing employees or their trust because we are uncompromising in our expectations. Compromises can always be made. If we really want to influence our employees, then sometimes we must make concessions. This way we build our credibility and make better progress in our impact on others' ideas and opinions. We should be aiming for a collaborative model and not a confrontational model. If we often find ourselves at odds with employees, it may be worth stepping back and assessing how we can change our behavior to impact theirs, and how we can manage the work environment to make it more reinforcing for them as we shape their behavior and teach them new skills.

What Is Shaping?

When we want to achieve a more complicated behavior we can use shaping. Shaping is the process of reinforcing small approximations of a desired behavior in succession to achieve the more complicated behavior. Behavior shaping can be used to achieve complicated behaviors that do not occur naturally or, as a behavior analyst would say, they are not in the learner's current skill repertoire.

Effective behavior shaping commences with a plan of the desired behavior and a detailed understanding of each behavior approximation to be reinforced. When shaping behavior, you start by reinforcing small steps and giving immediate reinforcement. The reinforcers are small and easily delivered so the shaping is not delayed.

Once the employee can easily complete the first approximation of the behavior then the trainer moves onto the next approximation, they "up the ante." (Chance, 2008).

The Human Component

Let us now talk about the human component of training. To be truly great trainers and coaches we need to understand how employees access, retrieve and handle all the stimuli we surround them with during our training sessions.

Here is a simple way to understand how we respond to stimuli using the five senses. Imagine for a moment you are sitting and relaxing in your backyard. You are capable of hearing for a mile or two, sensing an aroma from about 20 yards, touching anything within an arm's length, and tasting at a couple of inches away. If you were to close your eyes and then open them for a few seconds, you would be able to recall a lot of information about your surroundings, such as the color of the grass, trees, roads, birds, fencing, flower beds etc. This shows how powerful the human sense of sight is. Human hearing processes much less information in the same timeframe and our senses of smell, touch and taste even less. When we are training our employees we need to activate as many of their senses as possible. The more senses we engage, the easier the learning will be.

Each of our senses has different capabilities. In terms of learning, the two strongest are sight and hearing. Sight helps us process stimuli from the environment and hearing helps us connect words with visual concepts. Each of the five senses acts as a gateway to learning because every stimulus passes first through their portals and then into the brain.

When multiple stimuli bombard our system we are not capable of perceiving them all. Our brains quickly decide which are important and which are not. According to Stolovitch and Keeps (2011, p. 24), we are "hard-wired with an automatic ability to filter out perceptual irrelevancies." This is important to us as trainers because, when we are actively engaging employees, we need to understand and recognize they will filter out what we are saying if they feel it is irrelevant or nonessential. Our goal is to ensure that we not only deliver pertinent and relevant information but that our employees recognize this and personally connect to its importance.

During a training session, new information is delivered into the short-term memory area of the brain, which is not really an area at all but more of an information treatment location. This is where data is examined and, if considered important, transferred to the long-term memory. If the data is deemed unnecessary, it is forgotten. More often than not this process is not a conscious one.

Information that is not processed and moved to long-term memory can disappear within 15 seconds, a process known as *endocytosis*. As such, the short-term memory function both fills up and empties out with expediency. Short-term memory has been referred to as a Post-it note or scratch pad as new information is retained there only while it is being processed and is then used immediately. According to Mastin, (2010), short-term memory can be thought of as "the ability to remember and process information at the same time."

Research suggests the human brain can only hold between five and nine new pieces of information at a time. The "size" of the information is dependent on the prior knowledge of the individual. One might ask: Does an address count as one, two or three pieces of information? It would depend on the person and how familiar they are with the area. He may not, for example, need to learn the state or local area name but just the road name and house number. This illustrates why we break down our training tasks into small but salient parts and schedule the knowledge transfer over several sessions. If we pound information into people over a short period of time, it is probable many of the important bits are going to be dumped. This is a mistake I see many trainers make. In their passion to help solve their employees' problems, they overestimate their capacity to learn.

How does the long-term memory work? Think about your first boyfriend or girlfriend back in junior high, your first football match, your first date, or your first day at a new job. I am sure you can remember many of these in a lot of detail. This is the perfect example of what long-term memory means. As trainers, it is critical for us to know this because, when we deliver new information to our employees we facilitate its transfer from their short- to long-term memories. That way we will know, even in our absence, they still have the skills and knowledge to execute processes and procedures in the workplace. Bear in mind too, the longevity of a memory is sometimes impeded by our ability to retrieve it. Even if it has been stored, we will sometimes have to search to find it.

In my previous life as a regional training director, or a "train the trainer," I would often ask a workplace trainer to describe what happens in the average first training lesson with an employee. Almost 100 percent of them would laugh and start explaining or making excuses for everything they did in that first session, which often included the distribution of multiple handouts and very little hands-on training or structure.

The next question I would ask would be how many sessions it generally took with specific employees to train them on a new skill or task. Nervousness would once again set in as the trainer responded. In most situations, these self-confessions highlighted the fact that there is almost never enough allocated time or resources to theoretically resolve a skill gap problem or teach something new. This generates two problems. First, we are not resolving skill or knowledge gap issues with our employees. Second, we risk overwhelming them with way too much information too soon. As professional educators in private business, this often means we are understating the importance of our training services or short-changing our employees in regard to how we train and educate them, often followed by unfair workplace expectations.

To help employees grasp and retain information during training sessions, we can use different types of activities and tools. Below I will detail a few:

- Icebreakers are short, fun exercises that encourage employees to interact as a group at the beginning of team training sessions.

- Role playing can be a helpful way for employees to apply new skills and knowledge without fear of making a mistake in front of their own peers or clients. Role playing can be extremely helpful for practicing sales skills, conflict resolution or handling a client complaint.

- Using visual aids such as flip charts, PowerPoints or videos can be extremely helpful. As we speak to our employees during training sessions they will be forming pictures in their minds based on what we are saying. They think much faster than we speak. Therefore, providing the right and relevant visual aids during a training session can help create links between what we are saying and what employees are picturing.

- Fun quizzes are a great way to encourage learning and knowledge retention as they actively engage human competitiveness, collaboration and the motivation to win peer recognition, points and potential prizes.

The Adult Learner

Given that our employees work for us and, we hope, want to become functioning members of a productive and successful team, they are stakeholders in their own success. As such, they are often highly engaged trainees.

It is our role to determine what employees need and want to learn, how we can best teach them, and then work with them to develop realistic and attainable goals. In some situations our training may be mandated by a human resource policy, a departmental manager requirement or a corporate need for new skill development, but once we know the training goals, we can work on our strategy and how we will reach the endgame together.

The Trainer's Key Focus

Our focus as trainers should be on facilitating learning to help our employees absorb what they need to know so they can achieve their goals.

While children tend to be willing listeners once you have their attention, adults can be the opposite. Often they will need to see the immediate application of what they are being taught, meaning they may have little patience until they understand why they should learn this or that, and how they can or will use it. Adults also tend to be more actively in the here and now. To be effective trainers, we need to understand how they learn and how teaching them differs from teaching children. For many employees, their only teaching experience will have been with their own children and the concept of teaching adults may be strange and intimidating.

To get technical for a moment, adult learners are defined as people who engage in training either voluntarily or through the workplace. In the latter scenario, they have made a choice to work for you of their own accord. To compound the difficulty of teaching adults, you must also be cognizant to the fact that, in their own lives, they are likely to be competent parents, grandparents and functioning members of society. They may have joined your business after completing a successful career elsewhere or be in a transition period between one career and another. If they are new to your company, department or industry, they may be outside their comfort zone and about to realize this with a start when they embark on a training program. In this instance, they are *unconsciously incompetent*, i.e. they do not know what they do not know. Our job is to transfer the knowledge and skills that are essential for them to be successful in a way that enables them to draw on the information, store it, and make it available for retrieval when they need it. We also need to leverage and maximize any skills, knowledge and talents they bring with them from their previous workplace, career or hobby.

Our focus here should be on facilitating learning to help employees absorb what they need to know so they can achieve their personal goals, as well as those of the business. In some cases people will have been away from a formal learning environment for many years, and we may have to help them learn how to learn, i.e. how to assimilate new information and retrieve it later.

When we teach, we want to ensure the information is deeply learned and not just surface learned. When employees are learning, they actively involve themselves by critically analyzing new ideas and linking them to their existing knowledge. This level of learning leads to long-term memory retention and problem solving as the learning is generalized and easily transferred to new situations and circumstances. It promotes an understanding and application that can last a lifetime.

In contrast, surface learning is the silent acceptance of new information and a rote approach. Surface learning leads to shallow retention and does not promote a real understanding or a long-term retention of the knowledge or skills. This is of particular importance if you are training employees who work in customer service environments. Employees interacting with clients need to be able to modify and personalize skills and knowledge to meet the needs of demanding and dynamic clients. This ensures they can comfortably maneuver into any gray areas and still meet customer service needs while not compromising the financial or brand integrity of the business.

Teaching employees rote policies and systems does not allow for this, and can further frustrate dissatisfied clients when the service provider is constrained by guidelines and the inability to think outside the box.

Why Be a Supportive Trainer?

Supportive training environments prime students' brains for curiosity, exploration and learning.

To obtain long-term skill retention, we must refer to what is known as the *experiential learning process*. I have already referred to this in pass-ing, but we will now look into it in much more detail.

Anyone who has ever tried to do something new or learn a new skill in the presence of a critical onlooker will know how demoralizing, stressful and depressing it can be. However, being open to new experiences helps us learn by facilitating our brains to evolve and adapt.

As we become more experienced at our craft, we often become less competent at training others unless we are actively engaging procedural training skills. Why is this? As experts, we view our training tasks differently than our employees. We are *unconsciously competent*. This means we exercise our skills and knowledge so automatically that we are no longer aware of what we are doing. Therefore, in many cases, an expert teaching a novice can be very difficult for both parties – ineffective at best, and frustrating at worst.

A couple of years ago, a friend of mine asked me to explain the game of cricket. I love cricket and immediately felt passionate about the opportunity to teach an American friend about this fabulous sport. As a side note, so everyone can appreciate just how much I love cricket, I was the first and only girl ever to play on my school's cricket team, an achievement that, I believe, still stands to this day. In any case, a few minutes in to my fervent account of the game, my friend was already looking confused so I pulled out a sheet of paper and quickly began drawing the wicket, the fielding positions and explaining the rules. Confusion still reigned, however, until my partner walked in and proceeded to take over the teaching session. Within a couple of minutes, he had explained the game clearly, had maintained an active interest from his student and was now preparing the student for level two, the fielding positions.

Why Subject Matter Experts Can Be Ineffective at Training?

Be aware that subject matter experts process information very differently than their students. This is not always a strength in training and can sometimes be detrimental.

A cricket bat and wickets
© Can Stock Photo Inc./grgroup

Why had this happened? After all, I am a certified people trainer! Very simply, for two reasons. Firstly, I am a subject matter expert and therefore process information about cricket very differently than my friend. My partner understands enough about cricket to explain it but still remembers the challenging task of having to learn about it from my father. Secondly, it never occurred to me to explain to my friend that, in cricket, the batsmen do not have to run when they hit the ball. This is a concept that most Americans find hard to understand as they grow up watching baseball. Without that critical piece of information most of what I said made no sense. The lesson to be learned here is that it is not always best to ask an expert unless

"If money is your hope for independence, you will never have it.

"The only real security that a man will have in this world is a reserve of knowledge, experience, and ability."

– Henry Ford

they have a fundamental understanding of teaching or training practices.

Much of our expertise as trainers and business coaches has been built up over years of practice, experience, and trial and error. We will have acquired many of our capabilities through *declarative knowledge* (knowing what) rather than *procedural knowledge* (knowing how). At the same time we often find ourselves having to transfer knowledge to employees using context, examples and hands-on procedure, otherwise known as procedural knowledge. Research suggests that when people learn to do something or master a skill as declarative knowledge, it is not easily transferred into procedural knowledge unless the trainer has a system and process for doing just that (Stolovitch & Keeps, 2011).

Note: The final chapter of this book will provide a system of training you can apply in the workplace.

Fundamental Principles for Teaching Adults

For those of us who engage in teaching adults, there are some fundamental principles we should be familiar with.

Adults have had many years of being self-directed and are autonomous in their lives. They are likely to feel the need to express this autonomy in their learning process. As such, we should always encourage and reinforce employees to participate in the training sessions and, at the beginning of each session, cover what we are going to teach and why, and highlight the learning objectives very clearly. We need employees to buy in straight off the bat and let them see the immediate relevance of the session to their jobs. As we are teaching, we must guide them to understand how they can apply what they are learning to other areas of their lives. We also need to support the skill training sessions with important theoretical concepts that are targeted appropriately and without overusing industry nomenclature, scientific terms or unnecessary verbiage.

As part of the process, we need to focus on the *relevance* of what is being covered and how it may apply to other scenarios, and make sure it is directly linked to the employee's development goals. In addition, employees deserve *respect*. We should encourage an open and honest relationship so they will feel more inclined to discuss any problems with us. We must not judge them or make assumptions about their lifestyles or personal choices. Finally, *confidentiality* is critical to having a trusting and productive relationship with any employee. An employer-employee relationship cemented in trust and respect will help create an effective learning environment. Our employees are just like us, except with less knowledge and skill in a specific area (or areas), but with the common sense to recognize they need further training or education.

Training for Adults Must Be:

- *Relevant*
- *Respectful*
- *Confidential*
- *Motivating*
- *Engaging*
- *Personalized*
- *Flexible*
- *Reinforcing*
- *Retainable*
- *Constructive*
- *Structured*

It is also important for us to motivate our students. *Motivation* is the driving force that initially causes employees to reach out for help so they can reach their goals or perform at a higher level. It is an intrinsic need for people to feel safe and secure in the workplace, and they may also have a personal need to be awarded a promotion or more individual recognition. We need to encourage and manage employees in a way that inspires them to maintain a high level of motivation. Their performance will depend on this, combined with their individual skill level. As trainers, we can directly impact employees' levels of motivation by impacting how they feel about themselves, their jobs and our company.

It is important to make training sessions fun, *engaging* and relevant. Everyone will have their own individual and unique learning style and understanding this will help us find ways to reach them. Sessions should also be *personalized* to an individual employee's skills, goals and temperament. Even if we have a predetermined lesson curriculum for sessions, we must be flexible in how we deliver it.

The training process On Task Skill Coaching™, covered in the last section of this book, is suitable for any trainer but the timing and delivery of knowledge will need to be fluid and *flexible* based on each trainee. Remember, our employees are competent adults and need to have a level of control over their learning process.

How often do we see very skilled trainers being less appropriate and ethical with people than we might like, perhaps even bordering on punishing? Employees need huge amounts of continuous *reinforcement* during the acquisition stage of learning a new skill and we need to get creative in how we do this by looking for successes, highlighting progress and simply saying, "great job." If we are unable to reinforce people adequately or often enough because the successes have not materialized, then we need to lower our expectations and change the reinforcement criteria or reinforcement schedule. This means going back a level where they are more successful and thus earn more reinforcement.

We must also encourage *retention* of what we teach and the transference of these skills into real-life scenarios. This means our process must ensure trainees retain their new skills so they can practice them on their own. We must also teach context so they are able to transfer the new information from theoretical to daily practical use. We do this by providing real-life instances of how they can practice and incorporate each newly-learned skill and level of difficulty into their daily schedules. When possible, training should take place on the job and in the actual environment where it will be needed. If this is not possible, then we need to be creative with our training environment and our practice sessions. If we demonstrate only, trainees will be able to grasp the concept via their visual experience, but we cannot expect them to take this small practice session into a real-life scenario and immediately perform with competence. Instead, they need to see and experience demonstrations and practical applications. We then need to provide adequate time in our lesson plans for them to reflect on what they have witnessed, and discuss their experiences both during the training sessions and on the job. This can help them identify better strategies to enhance their own skill performance, and consider how they can be more productive.

Providing timely and appropriate feedback is an important part of the learning cycle and it is our responsibility to correct mistakes made during training with positive coaching methods. Our approach here will have a long-term impact both on our relationship with the employees and our future successes together.

Giving *constructive* feedback protects a person's ego while maintaining a system of training that has integrity. In many cases when we are training skills our feedback will take the form of additional demonstrations and follow-up questions to query the learning.

As professional trainers, it is important that we effectively *structure* sessions to prevent frustration developing. We can do this by providing ample amounts of reinforcement, communicating effectively with trainees to encourage their participation, and understanding their individual perception of the learning environment. It is our responsibility to moderate the task difficulty and take personal responsibility to ensure new skills and behaviors are tested before moving on to new, more difficult criteria. Professional trainers will always offer clean and unambiguous feedback. By being innovative in our training approach, we can ensure people are continually challenged at an appropriate level. In a nutshell, our role is to identify our employees' needs in terms of skills, knowledge and motivation, and then help them achieve these competencies by using planned processes so they can learn more effectively. At the same time, we must work to create a training environment that is conducive to learning.

> As Cozolino (2013, p. 244) so aptly states: "Our brain reacts in the same way to threats against the self as it does to threats against the body. Because of this, disrespect, shame and humiliation shut down learning as quickly as physical attacks."

Assessing Current Skills, Knowledge and Talent

In some situations, the knowledge an employee already has can be detrimental to their learning process as it may fail to support the new knowledge or be inappropriate within the context of the information we are trying to impart. When we begin working with someone new, it is important for us to understand what they know about the skills they wish to learn and what, if any, mechanical skills they may have. By doing this we can leverage their existing knowledge and fill in the gaps between what they know and what we would like them to master.

When people learn, they continually connect the dots between what they know and what they are being taught. Employees will also interpret the information we provide based on their own beliefs, assumptions and existing knowledge. Activating prior knowledge is an important part of helping them learn and retain new knowledge. Even if they have prior experience of the topic, it may not be sufficient to support the new knowledge. If we work on inaccurate assumptions or misgauge their competency, we risk assuming they know more than they actually do, and our starting point is likely to omit important foundational information.

Earlier, I mentioned the difference between declarative and procedural knowledge and now here it is again. Employees may understand some learning theory but that does not mean they know when or how to apply it to an actual task. In other scenarios, we may have people who have some very competent mechanical skills but, if asked to explain what they are doing and why, will not be able to provide the reason or theory behind it.

Many years ago I had a trainee who also happened to be a psychology major and a retired professor. This was a very difficult situation for me as he assumed he knew far more than he actually did about the practical application of his knowledge to the job at hand. It took a lot of patience and careful lesson planning to execute my curriculum in a way that worked for both of us, and I had to help him recognize he was applying his prior knowledge inappropriately. First, we had an open discussion and determined some ground rules for our sessions based on the premise of not making assumptions about current knowledge and its relevant application. Then we discussed that, like most science, learning theory requires a subtle amount of art to its implementation so we do not lose track of the fact we have thinking and feeling people in the equation.

As this case demonstrates, before we embark on any training we need to understand more about the participants so we can develop a successful program. To do this, we can take a three-prong approach so we understand what motivates them, find out what they already know, and establish what they need to know/learn during the program.

1. What is their motivation?

The answers to the following questions will help us understand an employee's motivation and predict how they will prepare for the training session.

- Is the trainee a new employee or an existing employee?
- Are they being trained as part of a corrective coaching program? Has the training has been mandated due to poor work performance or because they are being prepared for a promotion?
- Are they a rank-and-file employee, a supervisor, or a manager?
- Are you preparing for a training or teaching session? Will the information delivery during the session be focused on knowledge they need to perform their job, or new skills so they can learn to perform a manual function?

2. What do they already know?

There are a few ways we can gauge the level and extent of our employees' skills and knowledge without using inquisition tactics.

- We can ask them to show us a few simple things. While they are doing these tasks, if they can, ask them some questions or prompt them to articulate what they are doing and why.
- We can have them assess their own knowledge through effective questions or a fun test.
- We can involve them in brainstorming solutions for any problems they or their colleagues may be experiencing.
- We can chat with them about the subject matter to help them see their own biases.
- We can use customer feedback and satisfaction surveys to

understand how our processes are working in service delivery.

- We can receive and solicit feedback from their supervisor or manager.

3. What do they need to know?

To be thorough about our training program needs it is necessary to conduct a needs assessment. This may be for a team, individual, department or an entire business. For example, if an individual has been performing below standard and their manager or someone else in the organization has determined they need to be trained, take a few moments to consider and explore the reasons for the poor performance.

In any situation with employees, we should first assess and lay blame to processes and policy before punishing performance. It may be neither an attitude issue, nor a lack of knowledge or skills. Consider instead that it may be due to poor management, inadequate leadership, or a lack of clarity in a poorly-implemented standard operating or workplace policy. A *needs assessment* may bring to light more entrenched problems. In these situations, a broader training approach, or the involvement of management to address operating structures or policies, will be needed.

When conducting a needs assessment, the following steps should be considered:

a. Review the needs of the job. This should be easy if a well-written job description is on hand. If not available, this will be a good opportunity to develop one. Employees are evaluated based on the needs of the job. If the job needs are unclear, then it is impossible to ensure they are trained adequately and evaluated fairly.

b. Review the job task analysis. From the job description, there should be a list of the job tasks that need to be performed by the individual and to what standard. These should be documented in a department training manual. Each task will be analyzed based on *what* it is, *how* it is to be performed and *why* it needs to be performed to that standard.

Using objective criteria, we can review the gap between an employee's performance and the job task analysis. This will determine the training need. The training program is designed specifically to meet the needs of the employee, but must also meet those of their direct superior/manager and the business owner or person who invested in the training.

Understanding who is responsible, who is accountable and who needs to be consulted or kept informed is an important component to developing a successful training program. This is referred to as the RACI Model. This stands for:

Responsible	Accountable	Consulted	Informed
Who is directly responsible for the training goals?	Who is accountable to ensure the training is a success?	Who needs to be consulted before, during and after the training program?	Who needs to be kept up-to-date and informed on the progress of the training?

At the same time, we must take into consideration the needs of other individuals invested in the training. It is our job to find out the supervisor or manager's expectations and incorporate these into our program. The same goes for those who are financing the training or have allocated money into the budget. If we can meet the goals of the trainee, the supervisor or manager and the person financially invested in the training, we are more likely to achieve a successful outcome. These stakeholders may also have concerns about the program, the approach or, in some cases, the individual being trained. These concerns need to be aired and discussed before training commences. Once we have gathered the needs and concerns from the stakeholders and conducted a needs assessment, we can further analyze individual motivation.

Trainees have been described as having the mentality of a prisoner, a vacationer, an expert, or a learner.

- *The prisoner* is the employee who has been sent to training by their superior and sees no value in being there.

- *The vacationer* views training as an opportunity to get away from the grind of everyday work. They will be lackadaisical in their approach, arrival and departure times and program commitment.

- *The expert* is the individual who will challenge the trainer on every topic. They love the challenge and think they already know it all.

- *The learner* is the person who loves to learn and will absorb everything they can. They will ask lots of questions, arrive early and stay late.

Knowing which of these labels best reflects our trainees will help determine our approach. Understanding who they are and how motivated they are to learn, coupled with the training needs assessment, will help us prepare and provide them with the experience they deserve.

Helping Employees Develop Mastery and Competency

As discussed earlier, experts can be a liability in some situations and are not always an asset to the training process. Experts have a high level of skill mastery, i.e. a high degree of competence within a particular area of knowledge. Ambrose et al. (2010) propose that, for learners to develop mastery, they need a set of key skills they practice to the point of fluency so they know automatically when to apply them appropriately.

Developing Mastery and Competency

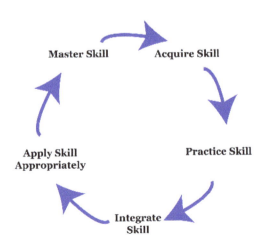

During the transition to mastery, trainees move through various levels of consciousness and competence. Ambrose et al. (2010) describe this as a four-stage developmental path from novice to expert. The four levels are depicted here:

The Path from Novice to Expert

1	*Unconscious Incompetence*	The trainee is in this state because he does not know what he has to learn. He does not know what he does not know.
2	*Conscious Incompetence*	The trainee becomes increasingly aware that he does not know what he is doing and that he lacks key skills.
3	*Conscious Competence*	The trainee has developed considerable skills but still must think and assess what he is doing as he is using them.
4	*Unconscious Competence*	The trainee is now very competent to the point of being unaware of how automatic and instinctively he is performing the skills.

We can now look at these levels in terms of our employees.

Level One:

When we first begin a training session we already know there is a problem, thus the need for training. In most cases employees know they need help because they are lacking a skill or piece of knowledge to execute their job responsibilities seamlessly. However, most of them are unaware of the extent of what they do not know until they are faced with the actual training situation. This is when they suddenly realize how much training will be required to get them up to standard with a new or existing skill.

Level Two:

During the first training session there is typically a lot of new information flowing back and forth. At some point during the first session, or shortly afterwards, employees begin to realize they feel incompetent or unsure. If this feeling kicks in during the session itself, they may become slightly withdrawn or overly serious. The trainer may mistake this as concentration. Alternatively, some employees may use humor to protect their vulnerability and others may come across as annoyed. Poor training delivery and information overload can expedite this feeling of inadequacy. If the trainer does not follow a structured training process or provide multiple demonstrations and exercises, then this adult – who is competent and functional in most, if not all, other aspects of their life – may begin to feel insignificant and unsure about their own capabilities. If people are left feeling this way, they are hardly likely to feel motivated to continue down the training path.

> **Keep Employees Motivated**
>
> *If an employee is left feeling inadequate or insignificant, they are hardly likely to want to invest any more of their time and effort into the training program.*

Unmotivated employees may retire from the training exercise or regress in their job performance – or both. The choice they make will depend on their individual resilience. If they feel demotivated at this early stage in the training plan, it will only create further setbacks. In such cases, we will need to subtly reevaluate the training program and approach while creating more realistic expectations. This can sometimes mean moving the goalposts to help trainees feel motivated again.

Level Three

If we are successful in our efforts to keep employees motivated and on task, they will become consciously competent after just a few lessons. In many cases this is where they start to feel a high level of satisfaction. Not only do most people need to master new skills or skill sets in the workplace, they actually want to grow and develop as it creates a more enriched work environment.

Level Four

To achieve or develop mastery, all the component skills at the various levels must be mastered. A weakness in one level will result in knowledge gaps and an inadequate foundation of knowledge.

As we work with our employees and they learn to develop their skills, they start moving from novice to competent. This means they not only know how to perform the new skill, but when and how to apply the knowledge in other contexts. To move people to a more competent level, we must present them with information and tasks that require them to use the skills to the point of autonomy, as well as enable them to transfer what they learn to new situations.

From Novice to Master

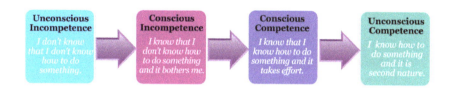

Practice Always Needs Supervision

If we explain how to do something, demonstrate the skill a few times and then leave our employees to practice on their own, we are doing them a huge injustice. Before we finish a training session, we need to supervise them practicing while we continue to coach. As trainers, we have a responsibility to leave them with assignments both parties know they can competently complete. Their job is to then practice and perfect the skill so they reach the necessary level of performance.

During the first few practice sessions of a particular skill, we must select and focus on individual criteria to help a person perfect it. If, while we coach them through their first trials, we attempt to correct too much at one time, no one skill will be mastered. It is better to step back and focus on just one skill. It is hard enough to multitask when you are competent but, for novices especially, this usually results in a lot of mistakes.

For example, during the first few minutes of training a new skill, a coach may focus on just a couple of things and choose to ignore others. By isolating individual skills and reinforcing them, the trainer can help an employee commit that task to memory, as well as experience quick and easy successes. I have observed many trainers set up a practice session and then continually interrupt with advice to correct all kinds of skill components. This is very frustrating for the trainee, who is denied any feeling of accomplishment or quick success.

To help with knowledge transfer, we must encourage people to apply their new skills as quickly as possible to real-life situations. If we effectively analyze what is to be trained and then present this in a hierarchy of component skills that ensures they master the preliminary skills first, there is no reason why they cannot become highly competent at the new skill.

Why Focus on Individual Criteria?

By isolating individual mechanical skills and reinforcing them, the trainer can help the employee commit that task to muscle memory as well as experience quick and easy successes. Break training tasks down into easily digestible pieces to make learning easier and more fun.

PART TWO
The Trainer/Teacher Role

What follows contains all the personal skills and knowledge I feel a trainer will need to complement the actual procedural training process. The procedural process I recommend is On Task Skill Coaching™ which, as already stated, is covered in great detail in the final chapter of this book.

Skill One – Formalizing Each Person's Role

When you begin a formal training relationship with an employee, first ensure you both have a very clear understanding regarding expectations before, during and after the process. You may even want to set up a contract with them, particularly if the financial investment you are making is significant.

In some cases, employees may be part of training programs that include third party providers and there may be grants or scholarship funds at play. In these situations, again there may be a need for a training contract that outlines performance expectations, financial cost and training results.

A contract is a business document that is legally enforceable. Your contract, whether it is an employee or training contract, should cover all the important components that detail the training scenario.

As a professional, you should hold yourself accountable to a code of conduct when training others. You should only consult and train within the range of your competency and, if necessary, refer employees to other professionals who can better serve their needs.

Competence is the measure of actual professional performance, not the level and amount of education. It is unlikely that professionals will be competent across all their business or industry interventions. Indeed, competent professionals only work within the boundaries of their knowledge and skill body (Welfel, 2009, p. 83).

A formal training contract, if it is necessary, does not mark the end of the employer-employee understanding. Once you have established formal guidelines for the training situation and each person understands and has signed the agreement, you must then consider the psychological contract.

In short, this summarizes the beliefs held by both trainer and trainee about what they expect from one another. It is an unwritten set of expectations that is constantly at play during the term of the program. The interactions you have with your employees are a fundamental feature of the trainer-trainee relationship. Each role has a set of behavioral expectations that are often explicit and not defined in the business contract (Armstrong, 2003).

The Psychological Contract

The psychological contract refers to the unwritten set of expectations of the consulting relationship.

Taken together, the psychological contract and the business contract define the consultant-student relationship.

Armstrong (2003) states that the psychological contract is blurred at the edges, cannot be enforced by either party, and is most often not written down. Yet this contract guides expectations, defines roles and helps interpret the relationship between the two parties. It creates emotions that form and control participants' behavior.

The essence of the psychological contract is a system of beliefs that needs to be articulated to the employee. In the absence of a mutual understanding of this contract, one side of the equation is going to feel disappointed at some point.

Expectations of the Psychological Contract for Trainer and Employee

Psychological Contract – Employee Point of View	Psychological Contract – Trainer Point of View
• The trainer will treat the employee fairly, respectfully and consistently.	• The employee will make their best effort throughout the program to learn and participate.
• The trainer will provide the employee a clear understanding of the scope of the work, time investment required and availability of the trainer.	• The employee will work towards a positive trainer-trainee relationship.
• The trainer will provide the employee with an understanding of how much involvement and influence they will have in the training process.	• The employee will be compliant once goals are agreed. • The employee will be committed.
• The trainer will keep his/her word.	• The employee will be loyal to the cause and to their progress.
• The trainer will provide a safe working and learning environment.	
• The trainer will explain role delineation between all parties involved in the training.	

When I review this contract with my employees or students, I aim to create shared meaning. I want both parties to have very clear and transparent expectations about our training relationship. I am very open with my employees and always highlight the need for complete transparency. I explain to them how I will share everything they need to know upfront so they can offer informed consent and agree to our plan of action. We discuss each point and clarify any misunderstanding. We put ourselves in a situation where, as from today, we operate as a team and make no assumptions about the journey we are starting, our motivations, intents or progress.

The points we discuss are:

- My role as the trainer versus their role as the trainee.

- What will be expected in terms of time commitment and effort?

- What each session will look like, how the student will experience it, how the training sessions will move forward and each person's role in these sessions.

- The time and energy that will be required to acquire new knowledge and practice new skills, much of it integrated into existing schedules.

- The training protocols, the philosophy and how things will work. We do not judge or criticize anything the employee has previously attempted. We are there to make progress and focus on the future, not to assign blame for the past.

- What is in it for each person? We begin to create a vision for change, a vision that each member of the training program wants to help create.

Skill Two – Managing Employees through Change

Once we have created shared meaning and the psychological contract is in place, we must understand what is about to happen. We are going to implement change into many facets of the individual employee's work life. In some cases, we may be training multiple employees in a department or across a business. These changes, involving new skills or procedures, may significantly impact and change the work environment for multiple people.

Preparing employees for change is very important and we will need to carry out lots of groundwork before we embark on the training. This involves being sure we fully understand what we are about to do and having a plan for how we will do it. We also need to recognize how it will be perceived and the impact, both positive and negative, it will have on our employees.

The first thing we need to acknowledge is that an employee's initial reaction to change will not always be positive. This is very natural.

Employees like to feel they are in control of their working environment and when we talk about change it exposes their vulnerabilities. There may be employees who feel the change is not necessary and those who are adamantly opposed to it. There will always be somebody in the organization who does not appear to have an opinion and who does not speak out. This individual is often the person who needs to be managed more carefully as we cannot combat and influence what we are not aware of.

> *"Change is the law of life. And those who look only to the past or present are certain to miss the future."*
>
> *– John F. Kennedy*

Even if employees buy into the change, or appear to, they can still experience frustration, anger, or both when they realize first-hand that their normal routines, habits, expectations, or behavior will need to change. They may lash out at this point or become uncooperative. As with any change, there will always be people who embrace it head-on and those that resist it. The latter is very common and stems from a fear of the unknown. If someone in the training process does not fully understand how things are going to progress, they may be intimidated by the entire experience, and if we have not shared our vision for the outcome with them, we are likely to experience some reluctance. This is where our positive and impactful communication skills will be integral to a successful change campaign.

What Should You Do When Concerns Arise?

If concerns or issues arise, we must take steps to bring about a change of attitude and approach. These include:

- *Engaging employees individually and seeking to understand what they need to personally achieve from the program.*
- *Helping employees understand that resistance to change can be a natural response, but we are there to help guide them through it.*
- *Orchestrating opportunities for employees who are advocating change to help those who are not yet on board.*

Conversely, some employees may just not care. As trainers, we must be wary of this. If the individual is indifferent to the situation, then they may not understand or accept it. Even when making positive changes, acceptance may not happen right away.

There are tools we can utilize to help battle any negative reactions to potential changes. For a start, we should always keep the lines of communication open. This will be an ongoing process that takes several weeks until the employees settle into the new routines. We may have to make decisions or change elements of the program on the fly so take the time to educate all parties involved about the reasons for this, and what the expected outcomes will be. Employees should always be informed of the reasons for our recommendations.

Employ Flexibility Tactics

Trainers must be flexible in both their thinking and their approach to employees. If they can, they will find it easier to generate a wider range of thoughts and responses when employees provide pushback to the training program.

Trainers will also find that, if they adopt a flexible approach to employees' needs, they are more likely to search for collaboration and not feel personally threatened by any resulting comments or critique.

In the meantime, we should be prepared for pushback. Not everyone will agree on what we are doing as they move through the program. If we encounter an extreme case of resistance, then it is prudent to provide that individual with some options that fall within the spectrum of the intended change. This should make them feel more involved in the process and help alleviate any negative mindset.

To gain ongoing support with employees, trainers need to identify the pros and cons of an option before making any decisions regarding the change process. Together, we must explore what is happening, what is working and what is not working, and always analyze opposing positions with

Provide Ongoing Feedback

To help employees sustain the impact of change, trainers will need to provide continuous and ongoing feedback for everyone involved.

care. If concerns or issues arise, we can take the necessary steps to raise awareness so we can rally everyone back around. Engaging employees in the process and providing a forum for them to express their questions and concerns is extremely important.

Feedback can feel very personal even when it is not meant to be criticism. In such cases, it is important to clear the air and not hold on to any bad feelings or grudges. As such, we must take the time to thank the employee for their perspective and for caring enough to take the time to talk to us. Remember, when employees give us feedback, they are doing so with good intentions. They are invested in the process and their goals.

Open, honest communication is the key to building relationships and demonstrating professionalism. While we do not need to discuss personal or private topics with employees, being transparent and honest about professional matters and generally willing to communicate with others is extremely important. People can usually sense when management is hiding something or withholding information and this can cause a breakdown in trust.

"You can get a great deal dwone from almost any position in an organization if you focus on small wins and you don't mind others getting the credit."

– Roger Saillant

Skill Three – Managing Employee Training Performance

Performance management is all about improving how we, together with our employees, perform as a team. The phrase "performance management" was coined in the 1970s by clinical psychologist Dr. Aubrey Daniels. At the time, Daniels used it to describe technology, the importance of managing behavior and the result of the behavior.

Performance refers to the accomplishment of a given task measured against a goal. In a contractual situation, performance is deemed to be the fulfillment of this contractual obligation. Between the psychological contract discussed earlier and the trainer conducting a well-planned employee assessment, we should now have a baseline measure for any skill, and a goal for the training program. Armed with performance management skills, we should be in good stead to help employees achieve the plan.

I always think of each of my employees and our training plans as individual projects to manage. Managing projects is a process: an activity of planning, organizing, motivating and controlling resources to achieve a goal. Employee performance management is certainly all that and more. We plan the work, agree on the expectation and manage the progress.

How effectively we manage the performance of employees as a team will depend on our evaluation process. It is not enough to implement an effective program that only covers the basics, such as new skills. We also need to be able to measure the progress and results. Therefore, goals and baseline measurements are extremely important. By having a baseline measurement and a good assessment system, we can keep track of a training program's success as it moves forward, allowing us to identify where any modifications are needed. We may, for example, have to tweak the program as new data is gathered. We may need to address the level of homework or amount of practice being completed in the workplace outside the training session. It may be a simple case of spending more time with one employee who is falling behind in their skill level. The success of the program, the employee and the system can all be positively impacted by an effective performance management system where there is an agreed upon set of goals and a strategic and tactical approach to accomplishing them.

Kurt Lewin, known as the founder of social psychology, introduced a three-phase theory of change that goes hand-in-hand with performance management.

Phase One: Unfreezing

This phase normally takes place during the shared meaning session and occurs when everyone realizes something needs to change. It requires all parties to accept moving out of their comfort zone to begin a new approach. Employees must decide if they are willing to change once they have considered all the advantages and disadvantages of what a trainer proposes. This is the concept known as *force field analysis*, whereby one considers the various factors that work for and against a proposed change in order to make a decision. It is important not to let people rush into a decision without being fully informed and offering their full consent. Employees who are not informed and have made an uneducated decision are more likely to renege on the psychological contract later, leading to frustration and heartache all around.

> **Unfreeze It**
>
> *If you want to change the shape or form of a large ice cube, the first thing you do is unfreeze it.*
>
> *To change it, you must melt it. Then, take the ice water and mold it into a new shape.*
>
> *Once it is in the new shape, refreeze it.*

Phase Two: Changing

Now employees are *unfrozen* and beginning to move, change can take place. This step, also referred to as *transitioning* or *moving*, is marked by the actual implementation of the change. This is when the transition becomes real to everyone as they experience, feel and see it. It is also the time people may struggle with the new reality. Because of the uncertainties of what will happen next, they can become uneasy and frustrated. This phase is the most difficult to achieve and it is my personal opinion that this is the stage where people are most likely to drop out or be assessed as unsuitable for potential promotion or cross development. As such, we will need to guide them carefully with a lot of support and encouragement.

Phase Three: Freezing

In the final phase, the new behaviors and routines become established. This is when we must reinforce and solidify all the changes that have been made, but it is important not to get carried away. Changes implemented once do not simply stay in place, but will require ongoing management, coaching and support. For those of us acting as trainers with no procedural responsibility for the employee in their workplace, we will need a system in place that can be transferred to the employee's supervisor.

Manage your employees' performance to success

© Can Stock Photo Inc./vaeenma

The *freezing* stage may only last a few days as we begin to introduce additional concepts and more difficult skill criteria. As we move employees through this process, efforts must be made to guarantee the changes implemented are not lost.

We will also need to review their performance. It is important not to leave feedback to chance or deliver it on the fly. Rather, we must invest the time to speak constructively to individuals about their progress, how they are managing as a team, areas that can be improved and areas that are on point.

Much positive reinforcement and encouragement will be required throughout the entire process. If it is necessary to discuss improvements or setbacks, we must take care not to do this in the workplace or in front of others. Instead, we will schedule individual sessions with the relevant parties so communication can be conducted privately.

We can prepare for these individual meetings by reviewing our training session history and progress notes and being very familiar with the program, the employee and their individual training process. If we are tracking measurement criteria, then it is necessary to have relevant documentation, know where current performance stands and, if we have a performance goal, know if we are getting closer.

If we are training several employees at the same time and session appointments are spread over several days or weeks, it can be difficult to stay up-to-date on who is who and what is what. In such cases, we need to implement a manual or electronic system so all our session notes, intake forms, goal statements and lesson curricula are at hand. This will make the performance management system much easier to implement and control.

SMART Goals

© Can Stock Photo Inc. / svanhorn

If we need to talk to employees about expectations, the meeting should always be treated as a priority. It is important not to delay because we fear it may not be pleasant and to schedule it so we avoid interruption. In these meetings we will always encourage positivity, communicate in an upbeat manner and use action words. We will talk about tangible goals with specific outcomes rather than emotions, keep the conversation objective and not allow it to become personalized.

If we find that expectations are not clear, this will be a good time to revisit the goals. Goals always show the strengths and weaknesses of a plan and its procedures, and implementing or revising them helps us understand where the employee's performance is and what needs to be improved. If we take the time to set goals, it is important to make sure they are SMART goals:

- **Specific:** Goals should have specific instructions. They should be detailed and not ambiguous. For example, if we are teaching an employee how to answer the telephone, we should be specific about the goal. There are different types of phone calls and ways to answer, and each one will have a different standard, process and output goal.

- **Measurable:** Goals should be measurable. Does the goal describe what the measurement is? Will it be clear when employees meet their goals?
- **Attainable:** Goals must be attainable. As trainers, we must not fall into the trap of setting goals with that are impossible to achieve. Impossible goals are not motivating.
- **Realistic:** Goals need to be something people can work towards. Given the employees' various positions and skill levels, are the goals set likely to be attained?
- **Timely:** All goals should have specific timeframes. Goals without timeframes are dreams. A timeframe applies pressure to get started.

It is important to remember that an employee's level of performance is directly related to their motivation, and motivating them is one of our key roles. We need to be their cheerleader. There is no single method or one-size-fits-all strategy when it comes to encouraging people. How we motivate them will depend on their personal aims and we must thus be able to understand them and the reasons behind their actions.

Skill Four – Managing and Resolving Conflict

Managing conflict resolution is a powerful tool

© Can Stock Photo Inc. / redrockerz

I wonder why is it that so many people have a negative conditioned emotional response to the word conflict. Why do we always assume that conflict is unpleasant, a creator of all evil? This is simply not true. As human beings, we are all individuals and it is when our differences come to the surface that conflicts can arise. I challenge you to switch paradigms. Rather than believing conflict is adversarial and aggressive, think of it simply as a difference in how people approach and feel about things. This mindset should make managing workplace conflict a much more positive endeavor. The fact that conflict exists is not a bad thing as long as we resolve it effectively. Conflict that is managed properly can lead to enhanced personal and professional growth.

Think about all the wonderful relationships we can forge if we view conflict as an opportunity to generate positive, collaborative solutions with employees, partners and business associates. In business, having a grasp of conflict resolution is a must, particularly when we consider how emotionally charged some situations can become. Once we have adopted the appropriate attitude towards conflict, we can arm ourselves with a conflict resolution process. This will provide us with the necessary tools to understand any differences with employees and interact with them in a more productive manner. We can greatly enhance the lives of our staff members if we are better equipped to collaborate with them.

> *"Seek first to understand, then to be understood."*
> *– Stephen Covey*

How do we define conflict? *The Random House Dictionary* defines it thus: "To come into collision or disagreement; be contradictory, at variance, or in opposition; clash." Some examples of workplace conflict may be:

- When an employee is dissatisfied with the look or design of workplace uniforms.
- When an employee is upset with his manager because she changed his schedule at the last minute.
- When there is a difference of opinion between the manager and an employee regarding how the workplace training is approached or implemented.

How can these conflicts also be healthy? Think about how conflict can increase motivation and competitiveness. These types of drivers can result in greater success, whether this is a better process, better teamwork or greater satisfaction. Everyone experiences conflict at some point in their lives. We cannot avoid it, so learning to deal with it is extremely important.

> *"You cannot shake hands with a clenched fist."*
>
> *– Indira Gandhi*

Let us look at this in greater detail. In the first bullet point above, we have a disenchanted employee. When employees are happy or neutral about their jobs, how often do we actually get the opportunity to spend quality time talking and listening to them? Most satisfied employees come to work, interface with their team members, do their job and go on their merry way so when someone has a concern they want to share, it presents the ideal opportunity to spend real quality time with them. If we handle these situations professionally, we will forge strong, long-lasting and trusting relationships, and employee dissatisfaction can be turned around. In many cases, employees who have had complaints handled successfully can become your very best team members.

The Process of Conflict Resolution

© Can Stock Photo Inc./vaeenma

Conflict resolution occurs when one party accepts responsibility for activating the process. If we sense conflict with an employee, it is up to us to do this. Before we can begin though, all stakeholders must agree that they want to resolve the situation. This means we need to sit with the relevant party, initiate a discussion about the existence of the conflict and then decide to do something about it. Without this crucial first step, it will be impossible to reach any solution at all, much less a win-win solution.

As soon as both parties agree a problem exists, and that they are both actively seeking to resolve it, we can begin. During the conflict resolution process, we must commit to removing and neutralizing any hard feelings, angry thoughts or negative emotions. Both parties should be given the time to vent and work through feelings associated with the conflict so the ultimate goal can be met.

Part of the venting process is to accept there are negative feelings and that this is normal. By acknowledging our emotions and their root causes, we can identify how to resolve them. The same goes for the employee. Once we have both completed this awareness stage, we can begin generating ideas about the root cause of the conflict and how best to resolve it.

Be motivated to clear up any problematic areas of misunderstanding. This will make conflict resolution easier for you to approach with your employees.

A skill I developed very early in my career was the ability to facilitate meetings and conversations with people that others found uncomfortable and difficult. As a young manager, I found it strange that more people did not want to resolve problems sooner.

In hindsight, I think I was more motivated to clear up the misunderstanding than I was deterred by the unpleasantness of the situation and having to approach the other person concerned.

"Conflict is inevitable but combat is optional."

– Max Lucade

A key step here is to recognize the importance of ground rules. These are important for any meeting, but for conflict resolution they are imperative.

Effective ground rules provide a framework within which everyone agrees to operate. The extent of the rules will depend on the situation and the persons involved. They do not need to be extensive or complicated and can be as brief or detailed as needed. It is essential not to shortchange the step of developing them as they are an important part of the process.

The ground rules for the meeting (or meetings) should be developed and agreed upon by all involved parties beforehand. We cannot just show up to a meeting and present the rules as this would be antagonistic and damaging to the process. Rather, we must be sure to document them and put them into a constructive context. We can, and should, make them positive. For example, rather than saying, "there will be no interruptions," we can say, "we will listen to each other's statements fully before the other person responds."

The ground rules must be fair to both parties, as well as easily enforceable and adjustable. At the beginning of the meeting, everyone needs to have a copy of the rules and take the time to review them together. Once the meeting commences, we can constructively refer to the relevant point in the rules if one party goes adrift. If working through a conflict resolution situation with an employee, we would be well-advised to take the responsibility of managing and monitoring the dialogue.

Sometimes, making simple statements such as, "I respect you and your opinions and I think it is important that we keep this dialogue upbeat and constructive so we can find workable solutions," can help keep things on track and build shared meaning.

Sometimes, making simple statements such as, "I respect you and your opinions and I think it is important that we keep this dialogue upbeat and constructive so we can find workable solutions," can help keep things on track and build shared meaning. Most people are not naturally rude, nor do they enjoy aggressive conflict. If employees take the time and energy to complain about their jobs, they have shown an invested interest in correcting what they deem to be mistakes. Employees who are invested are generally looking for solutions and this can help improve your business.

> *"Developing effective conflict management as a core competency can be accomplished easily with the Thomas-Kilmann Conflict Mode Instrument and can generate an immediate and measurable return on the investment."*
>
> *– Dr. Randall Wade, Rogue Community College*

In addition, if you ever find yourself involved in a conflict resolution situation with a mediator, it is important the ground rules are developed by the parties involved, and not the mediator. The mediator's role is to guide and mentor, not to judge or rule. You may need to politely remind them of this at times.

If you are the facilitator, it is up to you to provide expectations for how your meeting will run, and how participants will treat each other during discussions.

Here are a few examples of ground rules that may be useful:

- We will listen to each other's statements fully before responding.
- We will respect and solicit input from everyone at the table.
- We will work together to achieve a mutually acceptable solution.
- We will respect each other as individuals and therefore not engage in personal insults and attacks.
- We agree that we are all looking for solutions to meet the same goal.
- We will refrain from using inappropriate language.

Each person at the meeting can use the ground rules to monitor and modify their own behavior, as well as politely point out if somebody else violates any of the rules. The rules provide an objective and logical way of addressing personal attacks and emotive issues.

An example of this is: "Peter, I feel like you have cut off my last several statements. We agreed at the beginning of this meeting that we would listen to each other in full before answering. Can I request that you do that, please?" Ground rules ensure a level playing field and hold every-one around the table to the same standard of behavior, as well as help maintain fairness and avoid biases.

Let us now look at the five widely accepted styles or approaches for re-solving conflicts. These concepts were originally developed by psychol-ogists Thomas and Kilmann in the 1970s and it is important to under-stand each of them so we can use them appropriately. Knowing which style to use in each situation is an important part of successful conflict resolution. We are each capable of using all five styles and do not have to stick to a single approach. As individuals, however, we will often use the model we are most comfortable with. How we handle conflict in the workplace is a combination of our personality and the requirements of the situation we find ourselves in.

The graphic below depicts the five possible approaches and indicates how effective they are in terms of assertiveness and cooperativeness, with compromising sitting directly in the middle area.

The Five Approaches to Resolving Conflict

1. With the *collaborating approach,* all parties work together to develop a win-win solution. This approach promotes assertiveness over aggressive-ness or passiveness and is appropriate when the situation is not urgent, an important decision needs to be made, the conflict involves many people, or previous conflict resolution attempts have failed. It is not appropriate when a decision needs to be made urgently or the matter is trivial to all involved

2. With the *competitive approach,* one person in the conflict takes a firm stance and competes with another person for power. The first person will typically win unless they are up against someone else who is also competitive. This is a very aggressive approach and can cause other people to feel injured or stepped on, but may be appropriate when a decision needs to be made quickly such as in an emergency, if an unpopular decision is being made, or if an individual is trying to take advantage of a situation. If people are feeling sensitive about the conflict and the situation is not urgent, then this is not an appropriate approach as the resolution process should build collaboration.

3. When using *the compromising approach,* each person in the conflict agrees to give up something so everyone actively contributes towards resolution. Using this style is appropriate when a decision needs to be made sooner rather than later, or the situation is important but not urgent. If resolving the conflict is more important than having individual sides "win," or the power between both parties in the conflict is considered equal, this is a useful approach. However, we should not adopt this style if a wide variety of important needs must be met across the different stakeholders, if the situation is urgent, or if one person holds the balance of power.

4. The *accommodating style* is a passive style of conflict resolution whereby one party concedes so the other can have what they want. This style is not very effective but can be most appropriate in certain situations or contexts. We can use this style when maintaining the relationship between both parties is far more important than winning, or the issue at hand is important to one person but not really a big issue to the other. I do not recommend using this style when both parties are invested in the outcome, or if one person's accommodation will not permanently solve the problem.

> *"Whenever you're in conflict with someone, there is one factor that can make the difference between damaging your relationship or deepening it. That factor is attitude."*
>
> *– William James*

5. The *avoiding style*, not surprisingly, involves avoidance of the conflict entirely. By using this style, we are accepting decisions without question in order to avoid confrontation. We are also abdicating any responsibility in regard to difficult decisions and tasks. This method of avoiding is another passive approach that is typically not effective but can be useful in some applications. If the issue is very trivial or the conflict will resolve itself on its own in a timely fashion, then avoidance may be appropriate. However, if the issue is important or the conflict may get worse if it is not addressed, then it is best to avoid using a passive style.

Now we can look at the entire conflict resolution process. Conflict can come in many forms. Because it ranges in scope, seriousness and unintended and intended consequences, we may find ourselves using only some of these individual steps. In other situations we may use them all. There are some excellent individual tools within the process that can also be used, such as establishing ground rules for meetings and examining the root cause of the issue.

Conflict resolution with employees is extremely important if we are all to reach our goals. The following list gives an overview of the process. It can be used in any situation and is how I recommend anyone approaches and resolves conflict in their business.

Conflict Resolution Overview

Create an Effective Atmosphere:
- Defuse participant emotions.
- Set mutually agreeable ground rules.
- Set the time and place for meetings.

Create a Mutual Understanding:
- Identify the needs for me, them and us.

Focus on Individual and Shared Needs:

- Find common ground.
- Build positive energy and goodwill.
- Strengthen the partnership.

Get to the Root Cause:

- Examine root causes.
- Identify opportunities for forgiveness.
- Identify the benefits of resolution.

Generate Options:

- Generate as opposed to evaluate.
- Create mutual gain options and multiple option solutions.
- Dig deeper into the options.

Build a Solution:

- Create a shortlist.
- Choose a solution.
- Build a plan.

> *Forgiveness does not mean forgetting the conflict or erasing the emotions it created, but it does mean accepting that it happened.*

We discussed earlier the importance of neutralizing emotions and setting ground rules. Now we will cover other areas involved in the conflict resolution process.

Selecting the right time and place is key. Wherever possible, a quiet location that is easily accessible to all parties should be identified. Make sure there is enough time to go through the process without rushing anyone and minimize all distractions by agreeing to turn off cell phones. If necessary, communication systems should be forwarded to voicemail or placed on mute. If you are mediating a meeting between others, then be conscious of the needs of both parties when scheduling the meeting and choose a location that is neutral, one that everyone is comfortable with and that neither party has visited before.

You should be aiming for the model of win-win. You want a situation where there is mutual gain, which is the preferred outcome for any conflict.

To begin with, you need to identify what you want personally out of the conflict. Next, identify what the person you are in conflict with wants. Explore all the angles to maximize the possibilities for mutual gain. Once you have identified the wants and needs of both sides, look for the areas of overlap. These will be good starting points for establishing mutual ground and finding mutual interests.

In 1965, psychologist Bruce Tuckman (1977) developed a four-stage concept named the Forming – Storming – Norming – Performing model of group development. Its purpose was to show how teams can grow and develop together, but it can be applied equally to one-on-one human interactions.

Tuckman maintained it is essential for a team to progress through all four phases to grow and face challenges, tackle problems, find solutions, plan work and deliver results. The model describes how team members are very polite and welcoming when they first come together, and how they may descend into conflict while each member tries to establish their own position. From here, the boundaries are eventually (and sometimes indirectly) set and, if all goes well, the team will reach a place of stability where it can perform to the best of its collective abilities.

Most of the primary steps in conflict resolution are focused on information gathering and problem solving. However, both parties should strive to find common ground throughout the entire process. This will help each understand the other's situation and better position both sides to create a win-win solution. Positive gestures build goodwill and will help make the shift from two people in conflict to two people working together to solve a problem. It is extremely important to focus on creating positive feelings and energy. You can achieve this by adopting a good attitude, framing things positively, creating actionable items and trying to keep emotions out of your statements.

Develop Problem-Solving Teammates

Forming – establish clear objectives for the staff as a unit and for the individual members.

Storming – establish the process you will take employees through in terms of the training plan. Resolve conflicts and remain very positive.

Norming – step back and let team members take responsibility for their actions and their internal relationships.

Performing – once the team is reaching goals, you can step into a coaching role and become more hands-off.

While building a good foundation and gathering information are key steps to resolving conflict, one must also know what the problem is. Once the groundwork has been laid, it is important to look at the root causes. A good way to do this is to simply keep asking, "Why?" As you get answers, you can dig deeper with more *why's* until you eventually reveal the core problem, which can then be solved.

Forgiveness is another important concept. Forgiveness does not mean forgetting the conflict or erasing the emotions it created, but it does mean accepting that it happened. Successful conflict resolution should give everyone a sense of closure and a feeling of satisfaction with the outcome. Keep the goals in mind. Ask yourself, "Will resolving this help provide me with closure? Will this action help me accept what has happened and move on?"

Conflict resolution can be very hard work. When conducted effectively, it digs deep into issues and often explores unfamiliar territory in an attempt to resolve the core problem and prevent it from recurring. The process can also be time-consuming and emotionally difficult. At times, both parties may arrive at a point (or several points) where they wonder, "Is this really worth it?"

If you do arrive at a stalemate, remember why you are resolving the conflict. It can be helpful to explore what will happen if the situation is not resolved. What relationships will deteriorate or break apart? What impact will this have on the work environment? If this is a business conflict, what is the financial cost to the company? What will be the emotional cost to the participants? Who else will be affected? As far as our employees are concerned, sometimes just thinking about this is enough to motivate us to find solutions.

These questions can help you put things into perspective and evaluate whether the conflict is truly worth resolving. In most situations, it is well worth the time and effort. If you visualize the benefits, it can provide the motivation for everyone to work through the rest of the process.

Once you have a good handle on the conflict and what caused it, you can then begin to consider possible options for resolution. At this stage, the focus should be on quantity, not quality. You want as many options to choose from as possible.

> *"The difficulty lies not so much in developing new ideas as in escaping from old ones."*
>
> *– John Maynard Keynes*

You can start by generating ideas for resolving symptoms of the conflict and then move on to the root cause as you expand the list. Do not be afraid to throw out unorthodox suggestions or ask, "What if?" This stage is about what you can do, not what you will actually do. It is important you do not censor yourself or your employees, so you need to get creative. This involves recording all the ideas on a list or brainstorming diagram. Once the list is established, the time invested to build common ground and a positive relationship with the employee will begin to pay off, and the positive energy and synergy will increase, aiding output exponentially. In cases where it is difficult to think of a solution, you can ask these questions to get the ball rolling: "In an ideal world how would this conflict be resolved? How do we not want this conflict to be resolved? How might others resolve this conflict?"

You can now begin to narrow down your list of possible solutions and look at how feasible they are as options. This involves determining how much effort is required for each option. What is the payback for each possibility? Do you have a preference? Once all the conceivable solutions are laid out, it is time to move on and choose a solution.

The best approach is for each person to take a few moments to write down their individual criteria for resolution, then come together and combine the lists to create a final set of criteria. In this way, each party determines what they would like to do to solve the problem and what is important for them to do so.

The wants and needs of both parties must be respected. Once you have established the criteria, you can bring out the list of solutions and remove any solutions that do not tally with the combined must-have criteria. You should now have a small, manageable list of potential solutions. The next step is to identify and select the final solution or combination of solutions. This must be viewed as a win-win solution for all involved, where everyone's needs are provided for and all criteria have been met. Once you have chosen your solution, you can put it into action and move past the conflict.

Skill Five – Grasping and Using the Power of Persuasion

"Persuasion is clearly a sort of demonstration, since we are most fully persuaded when we consider a thing to have been demonstrated."
– Aristotle

As a company leader, business owner and professional trainer, I am reminded on an hourly basis how important the concept of persuasion is. To be an effective leader, you must be able to persuade. When you want to inspire and create dynamic change, persuasion is mission critical. As a professional whose role encompasses working through others, your persuasion competency often directly correlates to your effectiveness. If you cannot relate to these roles as an individual operating within a group, then think about how impactful persuasion can be in your personal life, for example, asking for a pay increase or resolving interpersonal conflict.

Persuasion is a form of influence. It is the process of guiding people towards adopting a behavior, belief or attitude. Persuasion is not about manipulation or coercion and it does not include deceit, force or dispatching orders. Its goal is to create and develop lasting changes in behavior, something we aim to do with our employees every day.

Effective persuasion requires careful preparation and presentation of ideas, supported by evidence, that are delivered in a credible and compelling manner. Most importantly, persuasion is not about robbing employees of their ability to make a decision or a choice. It is rather about impacting, engaging, educating and compelling them.

When we aim to persuade our employees, we must appeal to them in the correct emotional climate and help them see and understand why they should change their approach. Just as important, we must be credible and influential in helping them choose the correct door to open and which road to travel so they can get from where they are now to where they need to be.

"Persuasion is a governing power. Those who have it use it to their advantage. Those who don't have it let it run their lives."

– Paul Messaris

Can you identify with somebody you know who is an effective persuader? If so, what do you see? You will probably notice they have some very strong interpersonal skills. They tend to be good listeners. They solicit and give feedback. They are probably good people readers. They can sense what is appropriate and when it is the right time. They think creatively about the common good and are always prepared and empathetic. Good persuaders are very credible people. Their credibility stems from four personal characteristics (Janasz, Dowd & Schneider, 2002):

- **Trustworthiness:** a consistent, reliable, solid emotional character and someone who will look out for others' best interests.

- **Composure:** a self-assured and confident individual.

- **Expertise:** someone who has presented, even when passionate, reliable data and given non-defensive responses to criticisms and questions.

- **Appearance:** how one demonstrates over time, through personal interactions, a history of being engaged and enthusiastic.

If you want to persuade your audience, you will need to frame your point of view in a way that engages them, creates a vested interest from all parties and inspires others to "join the crusade." The best way to do this is to describe your position in a way that identifies common ground. This framing sets a collaborative tone to achieve three interrelated goals: providing the listener with the ideas you would like them to consider, forging an open way for alternative ideas to be compared, and creating a logical structure for decision making.

There has been much study on persuasion, and those interested in the research include the fields of psychology, communications and business. Researchers have proposed and tested several theories that explain persuasion and the factors that impact its effectiveness. Some of the findings suggest our ability to be persuaded is impacted by whether we like somebody or not, and by the amount of dissonance or tension – past or present - in the relationship. I personally like Reardon's ACE Theory Model (2001, p. 200), which focuses on three types of persuasive appeals. These criteria determine whether people will respond positively to a persuader, and all are effective tools when trying to persuade others:

- ✓ **Appropriateness:** this references the right thing to do, according to accepted standards.

- ✓ **Consistency:** this is how the action or belief compares to an individual's own past behaviors or espoused beliefs.

- ✓ **Effectiveness:** this is the degree to which an action or idea leads to a desirable state.

Note that there are some ethical and cautionary issues when talking about persuasion. When used correctly, it is effective in gaining positive outcomes for all parties, but when used incorrectly can be used and viewed as a road to manipulation. A quick litmus test when you are in the audience of a persuader or when using the power of persuasion yourself, is to ask yourself: Who is really benefiting from this? Is the information I am presenting being presented accurately? Does this interaction feel like a test of wills, a competitive game or is it a healthy and positive two-way exchange, a debate? (Janasz, Dowd & Schneider, 2002). We do not want to negatively impact our relationships by using methods that only work in the short term and do not create trusting and positive relationships for everyone's long-term benefit.

"Our minds influence the key activity of the brain, which then influences everything; perception, cognition, thoughts and feelings, personal relationships; they're all a projection of you."

– Deepak Chopra

Skill Six – Building Employee Commitment and Compliance

As professional trainers, we most likely have to negotiate with our employees every day. This can be about anything both parties have opinions on. Many professionals have trouble negotiating win-win scenarios with their employees, but being aware of some basic negotiating tactics can help us increase our employee commitment and compliance, enjoy our work process more and build solutions to meet everyone's goals.

In their classic book *Getting to Yes*, Fisher and Ury (1981) argue that most negotiations are not as efficient or successful as they might be because people tend to argue about positions rather than interests. Once parties commit themselves to a position, it is very difficult to move forward with sides arguing and further entrenching themselves. If you can become better at negotiating around interests, you will find many more positions to discuss and a lot more mutual ground to work with.

> **Negotiate a Win-Win**
>
> *Interest-based negotiating is not about a win-lose or lose-lose. On the contrary, it is all about win-win.*

Interest-based negotiating is not about a win-lose or lose-lose. On the contrary, it is all about win-win. When you are negotiating with employees this is the only way to approach it. When you are involved in interest bargaining, all participants become problem solvers. They then focus on finding areas of mutual interest rather than individual positions. The goal is an outcome that will satisfy everyone. Neither party has a bottom line, this is about mutual gain. Distrust is irrelevant as you work together to develop solutions.

There are three phases to a successful negotiating process. First though, if you find yourself in a situation where you need to negotiate with an employee, you need to prepare. This entails defining what you hope to get out of the negotiation, what you will settle for, and what you consider unacceptable. If, for example, you are having problems with an employee who is noncompliant with instructions, then you need to establish in your own mind what is non-negotiable and what can be negotiated to meet the best interests of all parties.

The key to preparation is to approach the negotiation with self-confidence and a positive attitude. If you do not prepare, you may end up acquiescing on important points. Finding the balance between acceptable concessions and getting the best deal for everyone relies on you being ready with a strong bargaining position. Negotiations are, after all, about the art of the possible.

> *"Place a higher priority on discovering what a win looks like for the other person." – Harvey Robbins*

When you negotiate with your employees about any workplace situation, they are often influenced by their assumptions about what they think the outcome or process should be. In some cases, they will have an unrealistic idea of what the possible alternatives are and may be unwilling to make any concessions because they think they can do just as well without making management mandated changes.

As a manager, you need to have a clear idea of your *worst alternative to a negotiated agreement* (WATNA) and your *best alternative to a negotiated agreement* (BATNA). You will negotiate poorly if you go into a meeting based on hope or false notions about what you can expect from your employees if you do not reach an agreement. When dealing with potentially difficult or sensitive situations you also need to establish your *walk-away scenario* (WAS). Once you have set your WAS, it is essential to keep to it. A walk-away scenario becomes meaningless if you are not prepared to follow through should the employee not meet the necessary criteria. Ideally, you are looking for the *zone of possible agreement* (ZOPA). This is where all parties in the negotiating process agree to meet to ensure everyone is happy and the relationship can continue to work towards its goals.

Proceeding through a Negotiation with an Employee

This graphic outlines the process of moving through a negotiation. During the preparation phase, you will identify all your key commitments and establish your WATNA, BATNA and WAS. You are then ready to negotiate. First, schedule a meeting and politely advise the employee you need to talk to them about the situation. As previously outlined, make sure you choose a location that is comfortable for everyone. Schedule the meeting at a time of day where neither of you will be rushed. Think about the environment for your meeting. It should not be noisy or have frequent interruptions. There should be privacy so you can talk without the fear of being overheard.

If you are conducting a negotiation at your own facility or office, you will have control over most of these things. If you are negotiating at an external location, remedy these conditions as much as possible before negotiations begin.

Once you have both arrived and the meeting has commenced, be polite but firm. Once seated and settled you can outline your position. Ask the employee to communicate their thoughts and where they are in terms of what you have told them. Present your commitment to the employee and begin to explore possibilities. Summarize any points you agree on. Be prepared to concede points if they are not non-negotiable. In closing, be sure to recap the discussion and what was agreed, then talk about where you go from here. What is the action required? How will you begin to move forward?

Here are a few tips for you to take into the meeting:

- Prepare, prepare, prepare.
- Leave behind your ego.
- Ramp up your listening skills.

- If you don't ask, you don't get.
- Anticipate compromise.
- Offer and expect commitment.
- Use positive words and phrases.
- Close with a recap.

Remember, you are always looking for mutual gain. When you and your employees understand the reasons for each party's respective position on an issue, you can find areas of mutual interest. Most likely you will find that there are very few competing interests and many mutual ones. Once you have agreed on these, it is much easier to find a place to start your discussions and get to an all-round yes.

Skill Seven – Employ the Art of Giving and Receiving Feedback

Giving employees constructive criticism can be one of the most difficult things for anyone who works in a coaching or training career. It is a real skill. When done properly and used with the intent of helping, it can be a powerful tool for achieving mutual goals. After all, employees should not only learn from their mistakes. They should also benefit from them.

A very important part of delivering constructive criticism is choosing the right time and place. During your On Task Skill Coaching TM training sessions may be too soon, but if you leave it too late the employee may no longer find it relevant to the situation. Let employees work through some of their struggles during a training session as this is part of the analyzing and reflecting phase of the learning cycle. If you jump in too soon to comment or give advice, you may shortchange them on their own learning process.

One of the best times to deliver feedback is immediately after a specific incident. This way the behavior or problem can be addressed right away. If you ignore things that concern or irritate you, then you are inadvertently setting the standard of behavior. Do not assume somebody else is cognizant to the fact they are being inconsiderate or doing something incorrectly. The longer their behavior goes on and the more time that passes after an incident, the value and effect of your feedback decreases. Think about how you reinforce your employee's behavior and the reinforcement history they are developing with regards to certain behaviors. Target the behaviors you like and feel are appropriate with heavy reinforcement. Meanwhile, redirect the behaviors you feel are inappropriate through effective feedback if necessary.

You will find it easier to deliver any form of constructive criticism if you prepare for what you want to say and how you want to say it. You need to specifically zoom in on the precise areas of concern, rather than address general problems. Careful preparation, clear delivery of information, and a sense of sensitivity toward the employee will result in a better relationship with them. Shared meaning and mutual understanding are powerful platforms to work from.

The goal of delivering constructive criticism is to help a person improve and be successful. Previously, we discussed how and when to use different tones of voice. During any session where criticism is being delivered, the tone of your voice must be carefully considered so it has the desired impact. If it is harsh or comes across as disapproving, the employee may either interpret your words as a form of criticism and be offended, or ignore and dismiss any helpful advice you deliver. On the other hand, if your tone is too light and amicable, they may not take your feedback as important or serious. Do your best to remain neutral and focus on helping the individual. Stay aware, so even if you are frustrated or nervous you do not become angry or use an accusing tone. This will counteract any help you are offering or the positive impact of the feedback. Practice what you want to say before your appointment and work on your tones and pitches until you are happy with how you sound.

Constructive criticism must be delivered face-to-face. Even in this electronic age it is not appropriate to communicate important and sensitive information over the phone or by email. Emails are usually one-sided and can portray inaccurate tones or contexts. Phone calls can be intimidating and do not allow for both people to feel comfortable or express their opinions or feelings. If you speak to your employee in person, then you know it leaves no room for misinterpretation. You can both speak openly with the opportunity to clarify any important points as you move through the discussion.

The Compliment-Criticism Sandwich

During your meeting, make sure you always use the *feedback sandwich*. The point of this is to offer coaching and support, while softening the blow of the feedback you are about to deliver. It is referred to as a sandwich because you start the meeting by genuinely complimenting the employee on aspects of their behavior that you appreciate. This can be an extremely effective tool if you do not use it to excess or insincerely. Any employee can feel – and they most certainly know – if you are not genuine or if your motivation is not to the benefit of all concerned.

Always prepare and outline what you want to say and follow up immediately with a positive statement or compliment. You can then present the facts about the issue in question before following up again with more encouragement. At this point, you can ask the employee for help in rectifying the problem. Having them participate in finding solutions will make them

Finding Shared Meaning

How can we discuss the features of anything when two people are discussing a topic in different languages? Ask any two people to describe friendly or rude and you will find they translate into many different meanings.

You must first seek to learn your employee's language and then help them to understand yours.

Utilize your questioning and inquiry skills to drill down and understand what the employee means by their words. Use words that do not antagonize or intimidate. Create shared meaning.

more likely to commit to the process and, in other words, find shared meaning.

During any conversation with employees, always monitor their body language. This will give you a good indication of how they are feeling and how your words are impacting them. If you use gestures such as furrowed brows, eye rolling, or stand or sit in certain positions that may come across as intimidating, you risk making them extremely uncomfortable. If they become unsure, anxious or uneasy, then they will not be able to actively listen to you.

If someone begins squirming in their seat, fidgeting or avoiding eye contact, you may have lost them altogether. If they are slouching, leaning away from you or sitting with their arms crossed, these can be indications they are shutting down. You will need to change tactics very quickly and try another approach. As trainers and "people experts," we should watch for the tiniest movements from an employee that may indicate negative emotions. Use your people skills to quickly assess how the person is feeling so you can temper your feedback. If you do this, you will become good at monitoring small gestures and will find that you notice very quickly when you need to change tack before people go over threshold, and become emotionally unable to focus on the task at hand.

Always check with employees to confirm there is a high level of understanding when you are discussing necessary changes. Encourage them to ask questions and give input on the topic you are discussing so they can self-check their own understanding. Reassure them you are taking the time to discuss the situation because you are heavily invested in their success

When delivering constructive criticism, always start sentences with "I" and express how the employee's actions affect you and your ability to help, rather than just criticize their behavior.

and the success of the training program. This way you can make positive changes together. Remember your active listening skills too.

When you work with employees to correct a problem, it not only supports them in making the appropriate changes to their behavior, it also strengthens the employer-employee bond. When people know they have your support, it will encourage them to be more committed, both to the program and the job. Always engage them to be a part of every solution to make them feel like they are really contributing. As a result, they will be more willing to make the necessary changes and improvements.

When you need to provide feedback to your employees, reassure them you are taking the time to discuss the situation because you are heavily invested in their success, and the success of the training program.

Feedback sessions with employees will not always be smooth sailing. Unfortunately, constructive criticism is often accompanied by some form of anger or negative emotion, usually in the form of denial or embarrassment. The goal of constructive criticism is to help employees grow and improve, not to hurt their feelings or downplay their efforts. If you deliver the criticism correctly and sandwich it appropriately, you should be able to manage the dialogue quite successfully and avoid it becoming emotional.

In the same way that our tone of voice can affect the meaning of our words, the actual words we use can portray blame, judgment or negative criticism. Avoid "you" messages that place the blame or problem directly onto the employee, such as, "You did not practice your new skills as agreed and then became angry with me for following up with you." Always

Avoid "you" messages that place the blame or problem directly onto the employee, such as, "You did not complete any of the homework and were angry with me for following up with you."

start sentences with "I" and rather than just criticize their behavior, express how their actions affect you and your ability to help. The correct phrasing can make all the difference when you are trying to deliver sensitive constructive criticism.

Here are some examples of incorrect versus correct word choices:

- Do not start sentences with "You." Instead begin sentences with "I."

- Avoid words that indicate you are angry or irritated. If you need to, use words such as confused or unsure. This will help keep emotions at bay.

- Express your personal understanding rather than your disbelief.

When we talk to employees there are usually many thoughts running through our head. Do not try to multitask as this will make you lose focus on the important points. Instead stay focused and on topic. If you have more than one point to discuss, deliver one topic at a time and completely finish it before moving on to the next. Sandwich each topic to minimize hurt feelings. If you try to combine several topics into one point of discussion, it will overload the employee and create bad feelings.

By the same token, it is not a good idea to throw everything into the ring just because you can. If you bring up problems from the past, it will distract from recent issues and confuse the staff member. If you failed to address earlier problems in a suitable timeframe, then leave them be. I would also recommend you try to avoid using the words "however," "although" and "but." These words can indicate that whatever was said prior, or by the other person, does not have much value, if any at all.

Before you begin to deliver criticism, stop and put yourself in the employee's shoes. Can you remember what it was like to be in their place? Remember how vulnerable and defensive you felt before you had your current level of knowledge and skills. Think about how people may respond to your words and how they may feel. Help them feel at ease by empathizing with them and letting them know you are there to help. Criticism delivered with empathy in mind is more likely to be accepted than rejected or considered hostile.

When I provide constructive criticism to anyone, I often start by saying something like (and I realize it may sound corny, but it is true): "I would not take the time if I did not care. I am invested in helping you. As a stakeholder in this process, I want us to win together. I want to work together positively and for you to get every ounce of knowledge and skill you can from me during our sessions together. I feel it is my obligation to help you be the best you can, and to help you be more successful in your job."

I am the same in my efforts to give constructive feedback to service providers. My partner once asked me why I provide feedback to some restaurants and not others. The answer is very simple. If I am not invested for the long term and do not care about their success, then why bother to give feedback? After all, it requires effort on my part. If, however, it is a restaurant I have a relationship with or one I want to forge a relationship with, then I will take the time to help them help me to be a frequent customer by providing constructive and positive criticism.

Skill Eight – Managing Employee Anger

If it is not managed properly, anger can be an incredibly damaging force that leaves professional relationships floundering in its wake. Anger is a natural emotion that stems from a perceived threat or loss. Employees can become angry if they feel threatened, physically or otherwise, e.g. if we challenge their existing ideas, thoughts or actions regarding how they should behave or perform in a work environment.

Anger affects the body, the mind, the overall emotional state, and individual behavior. Generally, expressed anger follows a predictable pattern. If you can understand the cycle, it can help you control both your own emotions and those of others. Anger management is an important skill for trainers as employees can become angry with themselves or others if they do not feel they are making headway in their training sessions. The table below outlines the various signs of anger:

Physical signs include:	Mental signs include:
• rapid heart rate • difficulty breathing • headache • stomachache • sweating • feeling hot in the face and neck • shaking	• difficulty concentrating • obsessing about the situation • thinking vengeful thoughts • cynicism
Emotional signs include:	Behavioral signs include:
• sadness • irritability • guilt • resentment • feeling like you want to hurt someone • needing to be alone • numbness	• clenching one's fist • pounding one's fist on a wall, table or other surface • raising one's voice • any act of aggression or passive aggression

The cycle of anger starts with what is known as the *trigger phase*, which occurs when the body prepares for a perceived threat. The changes seen at this stage are very subtle. Next comes the *escalation phase*, where the progressive appearance of an anger response becomes apparent. During this phase the body is already preparing for a crisis, which is manifested through symptoms like rapid breathing, increased heart rate and raised blood pressure. Once the escalation phase has been reached, there is less chance that you will be able to calm your employee down.

What follows is the *crisis phase*, where the body is on full alert and prepared to take action. In this phase, the individual concerned will no longer be rational, making logical discussion impossible. After this comes the *recovery phase*. The person's anger eventually becomes spent and you will see a steady return to normal behavior. During this phase, you may be the trigger for more anger if you intervene in any way.

At the end of the cycle, the individual may appear depressed, and they are, appropriately, in the *depression phase*. This marks the return to their normal state. Physically, they will have below normal vital signs, e.g. heart rate. This is so the body can regain equilibrium. They should now have full use of their faculties and may also express guilt and regret.

One of the primary functions of the human brain is to keep us safe. Involuntary reactions, such as blinking when an object comes too close to one's face or instinctively pulling one's hand away from a fire, are a large part of what kept prehistoric man alive. When we are presented with a dangerous situation, instinct dictates what we do.

The Fight or Flight Theory was developed by Walter Cannon in 1915 and refers specifically to how humans and animals react to perceived threats. It underscores how anger is a natural response and that there is no morality to it. It also reminds us of our need to stay in control. We can no longer be rational if we are angry. Instead, our instincts will lead us to aggressive and hypervigilant behavior, all of which are incompatible to a rational and deliberate response.

> *"In this world, nothing can be said to be certain except death and taxes."*
>
> *– Benjamin Franklin*

Because anger is aggravated by a feeling of victimization and helplessness, it may be useful to know that there are three options available when dealing with it: alter, avoid or accept. Employees are not victims of the situation. They have the option of taking a deliberate and well-thought response to an anger-provoking situation, as do you. If an employee gets angry, it can feel overwhelming and trigger intense reactions. Here are some tips on how to deal with anger more effectively. Each falls into one of the three categories:

- If you recognize that you have a particular way of doing things or a habit that can provoke anger, change your own behavior (*alter*).
- Respectfully ask others to change their behavior and be willing to do the same (*alter*).

- You cannot exert control over other people's thoughts, feelings and behavior. But you can ask them to change (*alter*).

- Analyze the way you view and react to certain situations and, if necessary, change how you respond (*alter*).

- Do not use irrational thoughts to govern how you react (*alter*).

- If your own anger is triggered by interactions with difficult people, then consider avoiding such people (*avoid*).

- One of the advantages of being aware of your hot buttons is that you can structure your day to avoid them (*avoid*).

- Immediately remove yourself from a situation that might cause your anger to escalate (*avoid*).

- Handling difficult customers sometimes leaves us having to accept situations that we cannot avoid or alter (*accept*).

One of the more delicate aspects of handling an employee's anger is knowing how to react without making the situation worse. This is where an understanding of the Energy Curve can help (*see diagram on following page*). The Energy Curve describes the typical pattern present in an anger response. It also details how reactions progress and how one might appropriately react at each stage.

The Energy Curve

The baseline of the Energy Curve is normal rational behavior. In this state you can still have a reasonable discussion. Once anger has kicked in the rational mind is no longer in control – you cannot reason with somebody who is getting angry. Anger builds momentum, a phenomenon known as the *take-off point*. How intense the anger gets will depend on the individual. Some people restrict themselves to angry facial expressions, while others will raise their voices and even progress to physical violence. This is definitely not the time to try to reason with somebody.

Eventually the anger stops gaining momentum and turns a corner. This is the *cooling down stage* where the person generally runs out of energy and, unless provoked, will begin to calm down. This is not the time to start a conversation or try to reason with them. You can offer supportive behavior but do not try to resolve the issue that triggered the anger. Only when the person is back to a rational state of mind should you start talking about the problem.

In the meantime, there are a few strategies you can employ to deescalate the anger and expedite the cooling down process. For the most part, an angry person just wants the opportunity to explain how they feel and have their feelings acknowledged. If you are genuinely listening to them, it can help reduce their anger. Be sure to create a comfortable distance between you. For example, if you are sitting too close, they may feel stifled. Ask if they are comfortable with you talking to them. Then ask what they think you could do to rectify the situation. Invite them to criticize you and ask what has upset them so you can understand what went wrong. You can guide the person towards taking back some control of the situation by offering some choices that may help solve the problem.

If you can find a way to agree with your employees, then do so. You can always agree to the fact that they have expressed their opinion. This can often deescalate the situation. Continue to emphasize your willingness to help. It sometimes helps to tell employees you are willing to listen but would appreciate it if they could calm down first. Remember, however, that not all angry reactions can be managed. There may be situations where you have to politely back away or reschedule another meeting. If at any point in time you feel intimidated or threatened, then your own personal safety must be the top priority. It is important to note that you should never reciprocate anger in the workplace with either customers or employees. In our roles as trainers or leaders we must always set the best example of how to behave during difficult and inflammatory situations.

Skill Nine – Benefit from Effective Time Management

Time management is, in itself, an extensive topic. Just a few months ago, I delivered two 90-minute webinars on this very subject.

> *"The only thing even in this world is the number of hours in a day.*
> *The difference in winning or losing is what you do with those hours."*
> *– Woody Hayes*

Even then I felt I had only skirted around some of the necessary areas. Time management is so much more than just managing time. It is also about managing oneself and one's employees in relation to time. It covers areas like setting goals and priorities. It means changing habits or activities that cause you to waste time and a willingness to experiment with different methods to maximize use of your time. In business, time is money, a perishable commodity that, once gone, can never be regained. We only have so many hours in each day that we can use for training so we need to make the most of them and allocate our time proficiently.

I will not cover all the necessary components of time management here, but will focus on those I feel are the most important. These are the areas I tend to see that are most in need of improvement in many of my employees or trainees.

One of the first things you need to do to improve your use of time is to remove all internal and external time wasters. A time waster is something that distracts or takes you away from tasks you are working on. These can be internal, for example, things in your office such as other people, emails and social media, or external factors that impose themselves from outside your location. These might include overly clingy friends, unnecessary emails or reactionary communications, where somebody else's poor planning seems to become an emergency for you.

Find the courage to remove or limit these "time thieves." This will help you concentrate and get things done. To manage your internal time wasters, you will need to develop new habits and some self-discipline.

Practice cutting or limiting the one thing that distracts you the most. It may be constantly checking texts or chatting to friends. Put up some parameters to prevent these things infringing on your time. You will be surprised at the results when you see how such small steps can improve your time management.

Pareto's Principle, aka the 80/20 rule, states that your results will come from just 20 percent of your actions. In most walks of life this is normally right on the nose. Ask yourself if you are focusing your time on the 20 percent of your activities that produce 80 percent of your results, or the other way round.

What is the Pareto's Principle?

A principle, named after economist Vilfredo Pareto, that specifies an unequal relationship between inputs and outputs.

Pareto's Principle (aka the 80/20 Rule)

© Can Stock Photo Inc./ivelinradkov

Managing time effectively means being able to choose what you do and how you prioritize it. This means you not only need to be efficient, but also effective. You should be spending time on things that are important, and not just urgent. Can you distinguish between the two?

*"What is important
is seldom urgent
and what is urgent
is seldom important."*

Dwight D Eisenhower

In a 1954 speech to the Second Assembly of the World Council of Churches, President Dwight Eisenhower, who was quoting Dr. J. Roscoe Miller, president of Northwestern University in Illinois, said: "I have two kinds of problems: the urgent and the important. The urgent are not important, and the important are never urgent." In his book, The Seven Habits of Highly Effective People (1994), Steven Covey popularized this so-called Eisenhower Principle with the development of a matrix geared towards organizing tasks, and the concept soon became mainstream.

Most people have a tendency to work on whatever has most recently landed on their desk, answer emails or focus on a specific task someone is pressuring them to complete. I hear so often from employees that they have no time to work on their own goals or projects because they are just so busy. They are so busy working on urgent matters that the important things never get done.

The Urgent/Important Matrix breaks tasks up as follows:

- **Urgent and Important:** Activities in this area relate to dealing with critical issues as they arise and meeting significant commitments. *Perform these duties now.*

- **Important but Not Urgent:** These success-oriented tasks are critical to achieving goals. *Plan to do these tasks next.*

- **Urgent but Not Important:** These impositions do not move you forward toward your own goals. Manage them by delaying them, cutting them short and rejecting requests from other people. *Postpone these.*

- **Not Urgent and Not Important:** These trivial interruptions are just a distraction. *Avoid these distractions altogether.*

The one complaint I constantly hear is, "I never have time to work on projects." Projects can often be so overwhelming it is difficult to get them started. Or, because they are so overwhelming, and if you do not have a time management system, you work on them from start to finish so the remainder of your business life falls into disarray. Think about behavior shaping, the tool we use to teach new behaviors that are not in an employee's skill repertoire (*see Part One – To Influence We Must Understand*). We may want to train someone in small steps to start making immediate changes to how they handle more complex situations at work. It is essential to break things down into several steps and not expect them to achieve everything at once. If we take a similar approach, we can teach people to work progressively on large projects and goals.

A Comparison of Important versus Urgent

IMPORTANT: *These are activities that lead you to achieving your goals and have the greatest impact on your life.*

URGENT: *These activities demand immediate attention, but will not contribute to long-term goals or activities. They are often a burden placed on you by others.*

First, divide the project into manageable chunks. Then you can block off time in your calendar to work on it. Once the time is allocated, make sure you stick to it. For example, when I decided to write this book the first thing I did was develop my outline. Then I scheduled four hours in my calendar each day to write. Because this was a very important project for me, I decided at the outset that nothing short of my office being on fire was going to interfere with the time I allocated. Here is how I suggest you divide your assignment:

- THE CRITERIA:

Break large projects into specific smaller tasks that can be completed in a set period of time.

- Allocate Time:

Rather than trying to schedule the entire project all at once, set times to complete the specific pieces. Schedule them when you function best. If you are a night owl, then do not schedule them at 7 a.m. Most of my creative work is done late at night as I function well then.

- *Plan of Action:*

Now, get it done. Begin each task when you have it scheduled. Do not procrastinate. Once it is completed, you will feel a huge sense of accomplishment.

Paper management is another area often overlooked when it comes to enhancing time management. I recommend getting used to handling one piece of paper at a time and decide what you are going to do with it before moving on to the next one. There are four ways to do this.

1. GET IT DONE: If a task can be completed in two minutes or less, do it immediately so you can move on to more important issues.

2. DELETE IT: If the material is trash or junk, delete it. Do not let it sit in your inbox muddling your more important documents.

3. SCHEDULE IT: If the task is one that cannot be completed quickly and needs action, schedule a time to take action on it and place it in the appropriate file until you do so. Make sure you tag it or use another follow-up system so you get back to it in a timely manner and do not forget it.

4. DELEGATE IT: If the task is not yours or can be more easily done by somebody else, then delegate it to the most appropriate person. This does not mean abdicate it.

Delegate versus Abdicate

Delegate = Entrust (a task or responsibility) to another person, typically one who is less senior than oneself.

Abdicate = Fail to fulfill or undertake (a responsibility or duty).

Poor email management is one of my pet peeves. I often attend online meetings or webinars where you have a view of the presenter's screen. The screen may suddenly flash to the presenter's email as they navigate their files. At this point, I have a problematic conditioned emotional response if I see their inbox is full of emails and being used as their time management/project management system. What does that mean? It means emails only get answered when they are found. It can become very problematic if employees are managing emails like this. As trainers, management tasks and workplace systems may also fall under our training purview, so we need to know how we can help our employees, through training, to become more productive.

To better organize email messages, you should have a good folder structure below your inbox. Once these are established, a folder and message hierarchy system can be put into place. This will help you identify the most important messages first and reduces the risk of you skimming over emails to handle something less urgent. I organize email folders by company, and then under each company I have folders in the same way I have any paper folders. That way I always know where to search for email I need. I have a separate folder for key people I correspond with. When emails come in I either respond to them immediately, schedule them for action in my calendar, or file them into the correct folder. The majority of time my email inbox is empty when I close my office at night.

Your inbox is not designed to be a storage area. When you receive an email, you do not necessarily have to respond to it immediately but the message should be filed away to an appropriate location so you can retrieve it later. If it needs to be handled at a specific time, then make a note in your calendar so you do not forget. If the message needs to be addressed by someone else, then forward it as needed and file the original in the correct file. In many cases the email is not needed at all and can be deleted there and then.

I guarantee spending time correctly handling email when you first open it will save you time in the long run. Important emails should not be forgotten or lost and it is a good idea to flag them or even highlight them in a different color. Flags can also be used to remind you of an upcoming event or project.

Like other routine tasks, email is best handled in batches at regularly scheduled times of the day, so allocate time each day for this. It is not good practice to constantly respond to emails as they can become a distraction to the other things you need to work on.

It can also help email management if you ask your contacts to use proper email subject lines. This will help you to determine whether incoming mail is business or personal, and urgent or not. Once you file it, searching is much easier if the subject line is relevant to the content.

Are you still using a paper calendar but carrying a smartphone? If you are using a calendar of any type to manage appointments, I highly recommend it be an electronic version that you can sync between your smartphone and desktop. In order to manage the many things you have to do, you need to have a safe, reliable system that you can back up.

Calendars can be used for allocating time for tasks, scheduling appointments, keeping track of projects and much more. Google Calendar and Mail are free and have some excellent features. I prefer to use Outlook as it allows me to keep tasks separately with follow-up features, plus it is a full contact manager and email provider. I can set up my emails directly in it and they do not have to go through a Gmail account or other third party web server. I can also back up the Outlook file to a backup drive. Outlook uses .pst files and these contain everything from tasks to emails and contacts, so back them up regularly to make sure all your information is safe and secure.

As we all know, there is nothing more destructive to our time management efforts if, when our computer crashes, we lose valuable information or it takes us hours to reinstall and update our files because we had no backup plan in place. With cloud services provided through Amazon, Google, Dropbox and many more, there is really no excuse to lose files or folders. Have a good backup system and one that works independently.

Skill Ten – The Training System

"You cannot teach a man anything. You can only help him discover it within himself."

- Galileo Galilei

The
SYSTEM
On Task Skill Coaching™

Why does On-Task Skill Coaching™ work so well? Simply stated, the learning cycle involves moving from experience, to reflecting, to conceptualizing and, finally, to integrating the actual skills. On Task Skill Coaching™ has been developed around this theory and is a practical application of experiential learning, the cycle of which goes as follows:

1. As we are learning, we first *experience* something new and immerse ourselves in it. We bring our own biases to the experience so we are caught up in our own individual meanings.

2. Next, we *reflect* on the experience. We begin to filter it through our own eyes based on our past experiences. As we move through this reflection, we can dismiss our biases and rigidity to see and feel more objectively what we have just experienced.

3. Then we *conceptualize*, at which point we narrow our focus from individual reflection and move from perception to concept. We seek to understand what we have experienced so we can label it or classify it in a way that makes sense to us based on our previous experiences.

4. Finally, once we understand the concept, we take *action*. For most of us though, action is not enough. We need to play around with the experience, tweak it and make it work for us. At this stage we have become part of the manipulation process. In other words, we can manipulate our actions based on our experiences, reflections and conceptualizations.

These four components are the cornerstones of professor of organizational behavior and educational theorist David A. Kolb's Experiential Learning Cycle. According to Kolb (2015), new knowledge is attained through a combination of perceiving and processing. Here are the four complete states in the cycle (*see graphic below*):

1. **Concrete Experience:** This experience can be planned or accidental.

2. **Reflective Observation:** Thinking about the experience and its significance.

3. **Abstract Conceptualization (i.e. Theorizing):** Generalizing from experience to similar situations.

4. **Active Experimentation:** Testing ideas generated from the experience in new situations. The cycle then starts again.

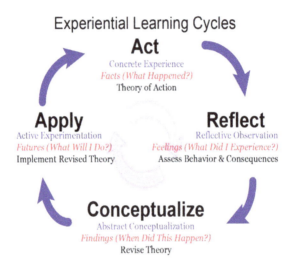

Consider the Experiential Learning Cycle as made up of quadrants. As trainees, when we move through the learning cycle, we ask the questions, "Why?", "What?" and "If?" Keep these questions in the forefront of your mind. We will discuss their importance when we review the On Task Skill Coaching™ process and learn how it all connects and intersects with the learning cycle a little later.

In the first quadrant, McCarthy (2006, p. 23) presents that we are answering the question, "Why?" At this stage, employees are discovering personal meaning and making connections based on their own experiences. They will also listen to you and share similar experiences they have had. In this quadrant, they think and speak at a subjective level, focusing on themselves.

In the second quadrant, people are moving from experience to conceptualization through the reflection zone. In other words, they are experiencing the *what*. This involves classifying, comparing, patterning and organizing all the information they are receiving.

In the third quadrant, employees are experiencing the *how*. They are beginning to move from knowledge to practical implementation, and are practicing and testing accuracy. At this stage, they are working towards mastery through doing, questioning and comparing results.

In the fourth quadrant, people can refine what they have learned and integrate it into their daily lives. This quadrant represents the *if*. Employees will be able to establish for themselves how they can use their new skills in unique and varied ways, and will be celebrating their new-found competencies and improved performance. This is exactly where, as trainers, we would like our employees to be.

Ultimately, when the On Task Skill Coaching™ method is executed correctly, it will help employees navigate their way around the learning cycle so they learn more effectively from their experiences with us, their trainers, and are better able to transfer everything they learn to their respective real-life scenarios.

Our goal is to impart as much knowledge to our employees as we can, supported by new and effective training skills, so we are no longer useful or necessary. If we are to do this, then we must be effective at teaching them to work independently to a high level of competence and remember that learning is a continuous process. Beard and Wilson (2013) maintain that "we do not learn from experience, we learn from reflecting on experience." Therefore, it is important during training sessions to facilitate the opportunity for reflection.

As we teach our employees, we must also recognize they will go through a process whereby they must decide, consciously or not, whether they want to learn by doing or by watching, and whether they want to include thinking or feeling as part of the process.

The graphic below depicts feeling, watching, thinking and doing at opposite ends of two continuums as they are considered dialectically related modes. To simplify the concept, the graph shows that learners "grasp" experience by doing or watching and then "transform" that experience through thinking and feeling. Kolb (2005) presents that learning takes place when this conflict between feeling, thinking, doing and watching takes place and is resolved by the learner.

The process of On Task Skill Coaching™ ensures trainees go through all four stages of learning so they can activate the skills and knowledge they acquire effectively.

The Simplified Learning Process

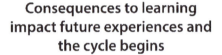

Consequences to learning impact future experiences and the cycle begins

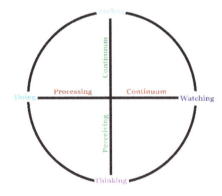

To summarize, then, employees' immediate experiences in the learning environment will form the basis for their individual observations and reflections. These are then refined into abstract concepts, with the learner taking on new information under advisement. This new information will be actively tested and used to form guidelines for future experiences.

Preparing for Your Training Lesson

As a trainer you have a training plan. This may have been developed by you or provided by your manager or a training department representative for you to execute. A training lesson is the period of time we are scheduled to work with an employee. Within this lesson there may be several short sessions on separate or interrelated topics. We need to make sure we run the lessons as effectively as possible. As a general rule, they should last no longer than one hour.

Before we arrive at the venue, we need to make sure we have all the relevant training equipment set up and any important documents ready. Preparation is essential. It is very unprofessional to arrive for a lesson and then realize that a key component or a handout we need to conduct it effectively has been forgotten. However, if it does happen, we have one of two choices: a) omit that particular skill session from the lesson, or b) train the skill without all the necessary tools. Neither of these is conducive to getting outstanding training results, however. I firmly believe that, if training is to be professional and effective, it needs to be done correctly, and that means having all the necessary tools and documents on hand and prepared.

During our preparation, we need to try to picture the actual training lesson and the planned sessions within that lesson.

- What are the individual training tasks we will focus on?
- What will we say, and how will we explain the *how*, *what*, and *why* of our training plan?
- How will we demonstrate the actual skill?
- What questions do we anticipate the employee will ask and how will we answer them?
- How will we handle any problems that may arise?

Finally, we must be sure we completely understand our material so we can competently demonstrate everything we expect the employees to learn. We cannot just wing it when training employees. This would be highly irresponsible and very unprofessional.

Quick Preparation Checklist

1. Have you prepared and are you familiar with the individual or group of persons attending the session?

2. Do you have your training road map?

3. Do you have your training plan?

4. Have you prepared your individual lesson plan?

5. How many skill sessions do you plan to execute in the lesson and do you have your skill sessions planned? This means:

    a. Do you know what you will teach first and to what criteria?

    b. Have you developed your *how*, *what*, and *why*?

    c. Do you have the necessary handouts to support knowledge transfer in conjunction with the skill training you have planned?

    d. Do you have all the correct equipment on hand?

    e. Are you dressed appropriately, i.e. do you look professional?

6. Is your training environment set up and any equipment you need ready to go and operational?

The lesson is initially dissected into two components:

1. What knowledge will you be transferring to the employee?

2. What skills will you need to teach the employee so they can perform the task competently?

You may need to transfer knowledge for each individual skill you will be teaching so you will not necessarily cover everything all at once. A training lesson may move back and forth between sessions and the required knowledge and skills for each individual session.

For example, in a training lesson on workplace health and safety you may have scheduled your one-hour lesson into three sessions. Each one will have its own knowledge to transfer and skills to practice:

Individual Sessions	Knowledge Transfer	Skill Acquisition
1. Correct seating at a computer station.	The physiology of the human body when seated incorrectly vs. correctly.	Practice aligned seating and correct posture.

2. Correct lifting procedures.	The mechanics of correct lifting.	Practice the mechanics of correct lifting.
3. OSHA* lifting above shoulder height.	The OSHA* workplace policy on above shoulder height.	Practice the use of stepladder safety.

*OSHA = Occupational Safety and Health Adminsitration

In addition, you must identify what supporting documents are required for the knowledge transfer and what equipment is needed for the skill training. In the above example you would need multiple tools such as computers, chairs, desks, ladders and items to lift. You would also need training manuals for the topics covered. These need to include all the handouts and any visual aids to help transfer the correct knowledge to the employee.

When training each of the new skills, what criteria do we hope to achieve? How much detail will we get into regarding workplace safety? Where will we start? What is the end goal? We need to define all these points as part of our planning. We cannot just show up to the session and plan as we go along. It is very important to keep accurate and up-to-date training records for all training lessons on all participants. This way, when we arrive for a lesson, we know where we left off, where the employee is in the training program and where this lesson plans to take us. Alternatively, some of our training sessions – such as any topics dic-tated by the Occupational Safety and Health Administration (OSHA) – are legally required, so we need documentation that the training has taken place, when, who participated and to what level.

WHAT IS OSHA?

OSHA is the Occupational Safety and Health Adminstration. It is the primary federal law which governs occupational health and safety in the private sector and federal government in the United States. OSHA covers topics such as hazardous materials, protective equipment, emergency action plans, and machine safety.

Before we begin any individual lesson, we should be very clear about what exactly we will be training and to what level. Using a lesson plan helps us to be sure we have all the necessary support and documentation readily available but, as stated previously, we may have three to five individual skill training sessions within one lesson, and we need to prepare for each one of them.

Each lesson should be conducted in the same way using the same training process. This entails working to the same method every time to ensure we guide employees through the Experiential Learning Cycle. There is a formula for this and I will now present an overview of the various steps involved, as well as what should be covered in each lesson.

Important!

Remember, On Task Skill Coaching™ is for each training session, so if you are covering multiple topics (i.e. conducting multiple sessions within one lesson), you will review each topic using this formula.

The On Task Skill Coaching™ system has eight steps (*see graphic on following pages*). The separate components of the *individual session* are as follows:

1. Open the session.
2. Show the finished skill.
3. One-way demonstration.
4. Two-way demonstration.
5. Trainee performs the task.
6. Supervised student practice.
7. Wrap up the session.
8. Assign homework.

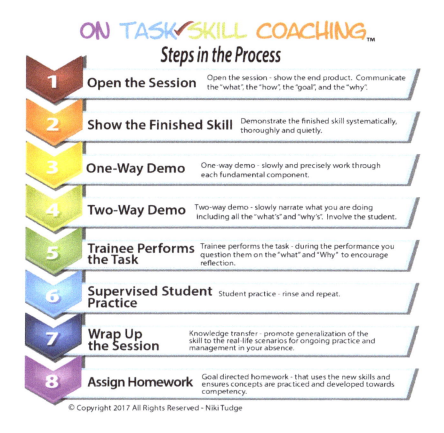

ON TASK✓SKILL COACHING™

Steps in the Process

1 **Open the Session** — Open the session - show the end product. Communicate the "what", the "how", the "goal", and the "why".

2 **Show the Finished Skill** — Demonstrate the finished skill systematically, thoroughly and quietly.

3 **One-Way Demo** — One-way demo - slowly and precisely work through each fundamental component.

4 **Two-Way Demo** — Two-way demo - slowly narrate what you are doing including all the "what's" and "why's". Involve the student.

5 **Trainee Performs the Task** — Trainee performs the task - during the performance you question them on the "what" and "Why" to encourage reflection.

6 **Supervised Student Practice** — Student practice - rinse and repeat.

7 **Wrap Up the Session** — Knowledge transfer - promote generalization of the skill to the real-life scenarios for ongoing practice and management in your absence.

8 **Assign Homework** — Goal directed homework - that uses the new skills and ensures concepts are practiced and developed towards competency.

We will now examine each section and its role in the overall process.

Step 1: Open the Session

The session opening gives the employee an overview of the plan and helps them feel comfortable. It should be obvious when we move from one session to another, and not just a blur of multiple activities within a lesson.

If the employee is nervous or struggling with any philosophical issues regarding the training, then we will need to address these first. For example, if we are training someone how to process a refund or a credit on a computer, this will be supported by the company's policy in this regard. The employee may feel the policy is unfair or inadequate and this may require discussion and an understanding first. We do not necessarily have to convince them our way is right. We simply must engage and motivate them to try. Our demonstrations and coaching methods will prove to them this is the best way to address the issues.

Most employees are nervous at the outset of a new training program, some more so than others. Again, we need to remember these people are highly competent adults who function well in society and within their family units. We must strive to put them at ease and use appropriate humor if necessary. For example, we may compliment them on their punctuality, appearance, or a new haircut. If we can find a way to connect with them, they are more likely trust us to support their first efforts.

At the beginning of each new session, we will introduce the skill we will be covering. It is important to be very specific. If we have formal goals for a particular session, this is when we will review them.

Keep this opening as short as possible. It may be as simple as saying: "Good morning (or afternoon). Today we will be continuing our session on how to register and redeem a client's loyalty points. By the end of the day, you will be able to fully process a client's redemption requests in the store."

During the opening segment of each session we will discuss:

- *What* we are going to be training. We need to create an expectation, paint the picture, explain the vision and generate interest and excitement.

- *The goal criteria* we plan to reach. This involves identifying where the milestone will be for this session versus the complete finished skill. Our goal must be tangible and clear: in this case the ability to redeem loyalty points worth up to $250.

- *Why* we are training this specific skill in this specific way. Adults, especially, need to understand the relevance of what and why we are training what we are training. There may be several ways to redeem points in the company computer system. One way might be quicker but may shortcut important client information, which will make contacting the client in the future more difficult.

The Individual Session Planning Worksheet

Step 1	
Open the session	Open the session. Introduce your session title. Keep it short and salient - just a quick introduction on what you are training, the goal of the training, and then briefly explain the how and the why (*see below for more information*).
Session name (*i.e. what are you teaching?*)	What is your session name and what is the employee going to learn?
Goal (SMART)	Specific, Measurable, Attainable, Result Driven and Timeline agreed by all stakeholders.
How? (*key method, philosophy*)	Explain how you will be training the task and what method will be used.
Why? (*relevance must be identified*)	Why does your employee need to learn this and why learn it in this specific manner? Make it relevant to them. Make sure they understand the *in order to* so they understand the output or goal to be achieved.
Notes for the session (*your thoughts and observations*)	

Steps 2 - 8	Items to prepare and have on hand	Sequence of events – key points to keep you on track
Step 2 Demonstrate the finished skill systematically, thoroughly and quietly *This is the finished skill that you have planned for the session. If it takes more than a couple of minutes, then break it down. You do not want trainees watching you work for too long as they will become disengaged.*		
Step 3 One-Way Demo *Slowly and precisely work through each fundamental component.*		*Key mechanics, timing and equipment to focus on.* This time you will do everything in slow motion so the trainee can see each one of your mechanics.

		What's and why's identified with each point.	
		What's	*Why's*
Step 4 Two-Way Demo *Slowly narrate what you are doing, including all the what's and why's. Involve the trainee.*		Each training topic	Explain why it is being trained a certain way and why it needs to be performed the same way.
Step 5 Trainee performs the task *During the performance you question them on the what's and the why's to encourage reflection.*		*What questions will you ask the trainee during the performance?*	

Step 5	
Trainee performs the task	What questions will you ask the trainee during the performance?
During the performance you question them on the what's and the why's to encourage reflection.	

Step 6	
Trainee practice	*Identify potential coaching points and how to address them.*
Rinse and repeat	
Coach	When you are watching your employee, analyze what meets the training criteria and what needs improvement.
Rinse and repeat	
Coach.	Improve and work on one point at a time.

Step 7 Wrap up the session *Knowledge transfer.*		*How will you generalize and transfer knowledge on this skill?*
		Talk to your employee about how they can generalize the new skill or behavior in different areas across their job. How can they use this new skill or behavior and integrate it into everyday situations?
Step 8 Homework assignment	What handouts do you need with you?	*What homework will be assigned (both principles and practice)?*
		What will you assign as homework? Make sure all assigned homework has been coached so you know the employee can complete it competently and that their supervisor is aware of the practice time required in the workplace.

Step 2: Show the Finished Skill

During this phase, we will fully demonstrate the skill up to whatever level has been determined by our goal. The goal is to demonstrate the finished product to the employee so they get an opportunity to observe and conceptualize what they are about to learn. If this will take more than a couple of minutes, we are planning too much for this micro session. We should not have trainees sitting or standing watching us for too long as they may become bored and lose focus and motivation.

Another goal during this phase is to show people exactly how the skill should be completed. If we cannot complete the entire session in 10 minutes, then we probably need to break it down into smaller components and plan more sessions. Remember, we can have multiple sessions in one lesson. I am not suggesting we could not cover this during the course of one lesson. I am suggesting it would be best trained in different or concurrent sessions.

While we are demonstrating a new skill, we need to be careful not to confuse employees by altering how we train it. This means demonstrating one method fully. For example, if there are multiple ways to do a task, teach one way first. Do not jump from one method to another as it risks causing confusion. We need to choose our method and stick to it until the trainee has accomplished that skill in that session.

When taking trainees through our demonstration, we must bear in mind we are not a mirror. It may be easier in some cases for them to watch from behind or to the side.

By showing the end result, we will motivate our learners to try the skill themselves. They will see how the behavior and or skill can be useful to them in the future and this can very quickly reframe the working context for them.

Step 3: The One-Way Demo

Next, we will demonstrate the skill very slowly without narrating each component. We need to let the trainee watch carefully, and follow these guidelines:

- Check we have everything we need on hand, including:
  - ○ Equipment.
  - ○ A client if necessary, or somebody playing the role.
- Position ourselves so the trainee can fully see what we are doing.
- Work slowly and methodically.
- If the trainee needs to observe from a different angle, repeat from a different orientation.
- Complete the full skill as per the goal.

Step 4: The Two-Way Demo

Effective trainers demonstrate twice minimum. Demonstrating helps cement the training in the working memory and facilitates the learning cycle. In the two-way demo, we are involving the learner. They are thinking and looking at what we are doing and should be engaged by the session.

At the beginning of the session, we will do a quick recap of what we are training in the session and why we are training it. Then, for each step of the actual mechanical hands-on process, we need to focus on the *how*.

When we present the various training tools, it helps to have a spare set so we are not passing equipment back and forth. Before we embark on the actual training process, give the employee time, if necessary, to touch and feel any new equipment they may be using.

For example:

A working desk or computer – it may be helpful to let the person sit down and become acclimated to the desk and computer position and location.

We will now demonstrate the exact same skill again, only this time we will slowly explain what we are doing, step by step. It is important to engage the trainee during the demonstration and, if relevant, ask them questions about what we are doing. We need to stress key points and areas of importance. Depending on the session, this could encompass topics like health and safety requirements or customer satisfaction components.

Caution: Avoid information overload. Training employees is not about showing them how much we know; it is about showing them enough to enable them to master the task. It is essential not overwhelm them with information, handouts and industry nomenclature.

The *How* Explained

During the second demonstration, we will get to the *how*. We will explain everything as we are doing it, and why we are doing it this way, paying attention to the following:

- Equipment choice.
- Cleanliness.
- Type of equipment.
- Body posture.
- Safety elements.

For someone who has not previously been involved in a certain task, it is important that we do not just train the end result but also the process, particularly if this is standardized for safety or branding purposes. For this reason we need to point out important standards as we model the skill so trainees fully understand it and the method of training, as well as why it is trained in a particular way.

If we train correctly, and explain the *what*, *how*, and *why* properly, then, even in our absence, our employees will choose to perform the new skills or behavior correctly and to the model we have provided. If lacking an *in order to* clarification, people may be tempted to take shortcuts or ignore important brand standards when working unsupervised. Students can thus perform their practice sessions correctly, which sets them up for success.

We must remember to communicate the *why* to many of these *how's*. When employees ask why we are doing it this way, we do not want to appear stumped if we have not thought about it or if we just do not know. Preparation is mission critical.

Step 5: Trainee Performs the Task

It is now time to have the trainee perform the task and practice what we have demonstrated. First, we take them through a review of what has happened so they can begin to evaluate the task after engaging in the process with us. We need to:

- Ask the trainee to describe the process they have watched in as much detail as they can remember.
- Ask specific questions about the process that we feel are particularly salient.

This will probably be the most difficult time for us as trainers. The trainee is going to begin practicing the new skill and we must try not to be anxious if they get it wrong or make a mistake. This is about the experience, and they need to experience the event to learn.

Making mistakes is part of the learning process, allowing people to further reflect and conceptualize what they are doing and need to do. If it is safe, then allow mistakes to happen to advance the learning. When people veer off course, we are going to be very tempted to jump in. We cannot. It can unnerve trainees and make them feel inadequate. We will only step in if we absolutely MUST, because what they are doing is unethical, harmful or unsafe to them or others.

If possible, we must let trainees finish the task first, but we must always be prepared for questions. As soon as they finish, we need to:

- Acknowledge they have completed the task.
- Describe to them in a very constructive manner what was done well and what we think could be improved upon.
- Ask them how they felt about what they were doing and what they achieved.
- Ask them what they feel they can improve on.
- Ask them about their overall experience.
- Recap areas needing adjustment. If there is more than one, choose the most important one to focus on in the next trial.

- ○ *Caution: We cannot tell employees that they did not greet the client correctly, that they forgot to follow a procedure, and that they did not file a piece of paper correctly then expect them to get all three things right in the next trial. First, it will just not happen and, second, our feedback will feel unsupportive and may be demotivating. We must coach and adjust one step at a time.*

- Rinse and repeat until the skill is solid and the employee can perform it seamlessly.

- At this juncture, we may choose to add another dimension to the behavior, such as distraction from other employees or questions from a client. By doing it this way, employees are only required to learn one new criteria, i.e. how to mechanically perform a task, before they have to perform it when they are with a client.

Step 6: Supervised Practice

We will continue supporting the employee's practice until we are satisfied they can do the task correctly and comfortably. During this time, we will be engaged in the process of observing, encouraging and coaching, and helping them make tweaks and changes to their technique so they can master the task. We may also need to supplement their theoretical knowledge and this may be the time to explain more theory so they can better conceptualize what they are learning.

Coaching is only helpful if it provides people with exactly what they need to know in a courteous and upbeat manner. To accelerate the learning of difficult components, we can have trainees practice problem areas in individual sessions. Their practice needs to be both goal-oriented and sufficiently challenging. Practicing is not just about time on the task but about quality. Trainers need to supervise practice until trainees understand all the moving parts. Incorrect practice will impede skill building, which is why it is so important we observe them doing the skill correctly before assigning any homework.

Step 7: Wrap Up the Session

The practice sessions are more useful if we wrap them up appropriately. This means talking to the trainees about how these new skills can and should be used in everyday real workplace scenarios. This facilitates knowledge transfer, i.e. the application of skills and knowledge from the training environment to real-life settings.

To affect transfer, employees need to understand the underlying principles of what we are training and not just the actual mechanics. For example, in an accounting office, we may train someone how to process a credit or a debit to the profit and loss account but they will still need to understand the principles of double-entry bookkeeping.

When wrapping up each session we can ask additional questions to help employees further evaluate and review what they have learned. Here is a list of potential questions for the review session, which typically lasts around 10 minutes:

- In terms of the skill we covered today, where do you think the next level will go?
- How can you practice this behavior without having to set up specific practice sessions in your workplace?
- Under what situations do you think you can use this new skill to benefit the client?

Step 8: Assign Homework

Training lessons in the workplace are often conducted by a specialized trainer and not necessarily the employees own supervisor or manager. After a training lesson, the employees may be assigned additional work and they will need to practice any new skills or behaviors as homework. Homework can be assigned from each individual session or the overall framework of the actual lesson. Remember, a training lesson – which can last an hour or more – will have several specific training sessions within it. The sessions are planned so employees are aware when a topic starts and finishes. If this is unclear, the trainer runs the risk of people becoming overwhelmed, with multiple things taking place and no clear goals and structure.

Homework is determined by the trainer and a decision will need to be made based on what is best for the employee, the employees' supervisor and the business. I only set homework based on skills I have coached trainees through and have seen them practice correctly. That way we both know, when I leave or we end the lesson, they have the full competency to practice and work the skill correctly.

I also need to be sure they can practice every day within the scope of their normal work. It is best if practice is goal-directed and has targeted feedback. This way it promotes the best learning gains and we can collectively achieve our training goals for the company, the employee and their working team.

Implementation

> *"If the first thing you do each morning is to eat a live frog, you can go through the day with the satisfaction of knowing that that is probably the worst thing that is going to happen to you all day long!" – Mark Twain*

The cycle of learning involves moving from experience, to reflecting, to conceptualizing, and finally to integrating the actual skills.

1. First we *experience* something new and we immerse ourselves in it. We bring our own biases to the experience so we are caught up in our own individual meanings.

2. Then we *reflect* on the experience. We begin to filter the experience through our own eyes based on our past experiences. As we move through this reflection we are able to dismiss our biases and rigidity to see and feel more objectively what we have just experienced.

3. Then we *conceptualize*, at which point we narrow our focus from our reflections and move from perception to concept. We seek

to understand what we have experienced so we can label it or classify it in a way that makes sense to us, based on our previous experiences.

4. Finally we take *action* once we understand the concept. For most of us though, action is not enough. We need to play around with the experience, tweak it and make it work for us. At this stage we have become part of the manipulation process. In other words, we can manipulate our actions based on our experiences, reflections and conceptualizations.

We can also consider the learning cycle as made up of quadrants.

In the first quadrant, the individual is limited by the boundaries of their experience and the resulting reflection. McCarthy (2006, p. 23) presents that in this quadrant we are answering the question, "Why?" At this stage trainees are discovering personal meaning and making connections based on their own experience.

In the second quadrant, they are moving from experience to conceptualization through reflection. In other words, they are experiencing the *what*. This involves classifying, comparing, patterning and organizing all the information.

In the third quadrant, trainees are restricted by the boundaries of abstract conceptualization and active experimentation. They are experiencing the *how*. They are beginning to move from knowledge to practical implementation, and are practicing and testing accuracy. At this stage, trainees are working towards mastery through doing, questioning and comparing results.

In the fourth quadrant, trainees are at last bound by active experimentation and concrete experience. They are able to refine what they have learned and integrate it into their daily lives. This quadrant represents the *if*. Employees will be able to establish for themselves how they can use their new skills in unique and varied ways and will be celebrating their new-found competencies and improved performance. This is exactly where, as trainers, we would like our students to be.

The chart on the following page demonstrates how On Task Skill Coaching™ meets the Experiential Learning Cycle. It shows how students move around the learning cycle as they go through each of the eight steps in the On-Task Skill Coaching™ process.

Ultimately, when the On-Task Skill Coaching™ method is executed correctly, it will help students navigate their way around the learning cycle so they learn more effectively from their experiences with you, the trainer, and are better able to transfer everything they have learned to their respective real life scenarios.

By implementing this simple and effective system, you can become a highly effective people trainer. You will be overjoyed by the results you see, results that will positively impact the lives of your employees.

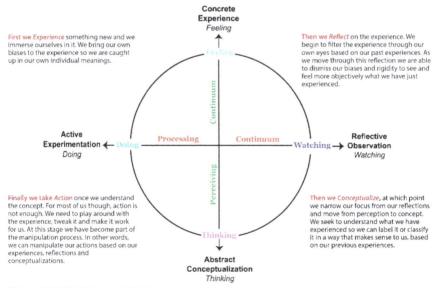

The Individual Training Sessions
On Task Skill Coaching Meets the Learning Cycle

The cycle of learning involves moving from experience, to reflecting, to conceptualizing, and finally to integrating the actual skills.

Concrete Experience
Feeling

First we *Experience* something new and we immerse ourselves in it. We bring our own biases to the experience so we are caught up in our own individual meanings.

Then we *Reflect* on the experience. We begin to filter the experience through our own eyes based on our past experiences. As we move through this reflection we are able to dismiss our biases and rigidity to see and feel more objectively what we have just experienced.

Active Experimentation
Doing

Processing Continuum

Reflective Observation
Watching

Finally we take *Action* once we understand the concept. For most of us though, action is not enough. We need to play around with the experience, tweak it and make it work for us. At this stage we have become part of the manipulation process. In other words, we can manipulate our actions based on our experiences, reflections and conceptualizations.

Then we *Conceptualize*, at which point we narrow our focus from our reflections and move from perception to concept. We seek to understand what we have experienced so we can label it or classify it in a way that makes sense to us, based on our previous experiences.

Abstract Conceptualization
Thinking

References

Armstrong, M. (2003). Human Resource Development. 9th edn. Kogan Page. London, UK.

Ambrose, S. A., Bridges, M.W., Lovett, M.C., DiPietro, M., & Norman, M.K. (2010). How Learning Works. Jossey Bass, Inc. San Francisco, CA.

Beard, C., & Wilson, J.P. (2013). Experiential Learning. A Handbook for Education, Training and Coaching. 3rd edn. Kogan Page. London, UK.

Buckingham M., & Coffman, C. (1999). First Break All the Rules. Simon & Schuster. New York, NY.

Chance, P. (2008). Learning and Behavior. Wadsworth Cengage Learning. Belmont, CA.

Cozolino, L. (2013). The Social Neuroscience of Education. Norton & Company. New York, NY & London, UK.

De Janasz, S.C., Dowd, K., & Schneider, B. Z. (2002). Interpersonal Skills in Organizations. McGraw-Hill. New York, NY.

Kolb, D. A. (2015). Experiential Leaning. 2nd edn. Pearson Education Inc. Upper Saddle River, NJ.

Martinetz, C. F. PhD Appreciative Inquiry as an Organizational Development Tool. Available from: from <https://appreciativeinquiry.case.edu/uploads/AI%20as%20OD%20Tool-Martinetz.pdf (25th April 2017).

Mastin, L. (2010). Short Term Working Memory. Available from: <http://www.human-memory.net/types_short.html> [April 13, 2017].

McCarthy, B., & McCarthy, D. (2006). Teaching Around the 4MAT Cycle. Corwin Press. Thousand Oaks, CA.

Pande, S., Neuman, R.P., & Cavanagh, R.P. (2000). The Six Sigma Way: How

GE, Motorola, and Other Top Companies are Honing Their Performance. McGraw Hill. New York, NY.

Pierce, D.W., & Cheney, C.D. (2004). Behavior Analysis and Learning. Lawrence Erlbaum Associates, Inc. Mahwah, NJ.

Pollice, G. (2003). Teaching versus Training. *The Rational Edge Publication*. Available from: <http://www.ibm.com/developerworks/rational/library/content/RationalEdge/mar04/3810.pdf> [15 August 2015].

Rao, M.S. (2008). Teaching versus Training. Available from: <http://profmsr.blogspot.com/2008/08/teaching-vs-training.html> [15 August 2015].

Rogers, A. (2003). What is the Difference? A new critique of adult learning and teaching. NIACE. Leicester, UK.

Reardon, K.K. (2001). The Secret Handshake: Mastering the Politics of the Business Inner Circle. Doubleday. New York, NY.

Stolovitch, H.D., & Keeps, E. J. (2011). Telling Ain't Training. 2nd edn. ASTD Press. Danvers, MA.

Smith, M. K. (2005). Bruce W. Tuckman - forming, storming, norming and performing in groups, *the encyclopedia of informal education*. Available from: <http://infed.org/mobi/bruce-w-tuckman-forming-storming-norming-and-performing-in-groups> [15 August 2015].

Tuckman, B.W., & Jensen, M.A.C. (1977, December). Stages of Small Group Development Revisited. *Group & Organization Studies* (pre-1986) 2 4 ABI/INFORM Global p. 419. Available from: <http://www.freewebs.com/group-management/BruceTuckman(1).pdf > [27 July 2015].

Ury, W. L., & Fischer, R. (1981). Getting To Yes. 3rd edn. Penguin Publishing. London, UK.

Welfel, E.R. (2009). Ethics in Counseling and Psychotherapy. 4th edn. Cengage Learning. Boston, MA.

Wolvin, A.D. (1983). Improving Listening Skills. In *Improving Speaking and Listening Skills. New Directions for College Learning Assistance*, ed. Rubin, R. B., vol. 12. Jossey-Bass, Inc. San Francisco, CA.

Lightning Source UK Ltd.
Milton Keynes UK
UKHW051944270219

338150UK00006B/232/P